High-Functioning Classrooms

High-Functioning Classrooms

Improving the Delivery Skills of PK–12 Teachers

Mark A. Marchese

ROWMAN & LITTLEFIELD
Lanham • Boulder • New York • London

Published by Rowman & Littlefield
An imprint of The Rowman & Littlefield Publishing Group, Inc.
4501 Forbes Boulevard, Suite 200, Lanham, Maryland 20706
www.rowman.com

86-90 Paul Street, London EC2A 4NE

Copyright © 2024 by Applied Teaching Projects, LLC

All rights reserved. No part of this book may be reproduced in any form or by any electronic or mechanical means, including information storage and retrieval systems, without written permission from the publisher, except by a reviewer who may quote passages in a review.

British Library Cataloguing in Publication Information Available

Library of Congress Cataloging-in-Publication Data

Library of Congress Cataloging-in-Publication DataNames: Marchese, Mark A., author.
Title: High-functioning classrooms : improving the delivery skills of PK–12 teachers / Mark A. Marchese.
Description: Lanham, Maryland : Rowman & Littlefield, [2023] | Summary: "Designed to improve the organizational, planning, and instructional delivery skills of PK-12 classroom teachers, the approach and flow of the book takes classroom teachers through a chronological sequence of what to expect, how to properly prepare for such expected events, and how to learn from those experiences"-- Provided by publisher.
Identifiers: LCCN 2023034258 (print) | LCCN 2023034259 (ebook) | ISBN 9781475873528 (cloth) | ISBN 9781475873535 (paperback : acid-free paper) | ISBN 9781475873542 (ebook)
Subjects: LCSH: Effective teaching--United States. | Teachers--In-service training--United States.
Classification: LCC LB1025.3 .M3371137 2023 (print) | LCC LB1025.3 (ebook) | DDC 371.102--dc23/eng/20230819
LC record available at https://lccn.loc.gov/2023034258
LC ebook record available at https://lccn.loc.gov/2023034259

This book is dedicated to my wife, Cindy Marchese, for her comprehensive and unwavering support of me and my teaching career over the last six decades.

Contents

Preface ix

Chapter 1: Establishing a Personal Philosophy of Instruction and Classroom Climate Policies 1

Chapter 2: Understanding Your Community and Student Population 9

Chapter 3: Preparing a Classroom for a New Academic Year 17

Chapter 4: Knowing the Curriculum and What Is Expected of You 33

Chapter 5: The First Steps of Planning Instruction 39

Chapter 6: Planning Instruction for a New Academic Year 45

Chapter 7: Planning Weekly Instruction 55

Chapter 8: Planning Daily Instruction 63

Chapter 9: Creating a Productive Classroom Learning Environment 75

Chapter 10: Teacher–Parent Communications 93

Chapter 11: Maintaining High Professional Standards 103

Chapter 12: The End of the School Year and Taking Care of Yourself 109

Appendix: Scenarios for Reflection 113
Index 121
About the Author 125

Preface

Knowledge not shared is knowledge wasted.

—J. M. Cornwell

From an early age I have always placed a premium on organization. Perhaps this was a compensatory device that I developed to counter my own attention deficit issues, to which I will admit. A large part of my long running and personal "war on disorganization" was writing things down. For decades I have filled out notebooks, folders, files, calendar books, composition books, and loose-leaf papers with written plans, models, schema, notes, memos, lists, poetry, and thoughts. This process reached its apex in undergraduate work when I would transcribe up to twelve pages of notes in a fifty-minute class, return home and summarize them into one side of one page, and then memorize that page. I would repeat this process after each class session and then review in a cumulative fashion. By a term's end I had taken well over a hundred pages of notes and had condensed them into twelve pages that were fully memorized. I prided myself on the fact that any further study for final exams would be a redundancy. I had a feeling of accomplishment, as if I had achieved a mastery of something, in this case it was the college style of "learning" as the professor taught, take and pass the test, and get an A. Later, as a first-year teacher, I continued my note-taking habit and stored the pages in the top right-hand drawer of my desk. Being an individual of high physical and mental energy, I found the classroom to be the perfect outlet and environment for inventive as well as reflective thought. *What do I want to try next with the students?* Take notes and put them in the drawer. *Did this activity engage the students?* Take notes and put them in the drawer. *How can I refine this lesson to make it better?* Take notes and put them in the drawer. *How can I improve my grading system?* Take notes and put them in the drawer. *How did the parents respond to this classroom policy or practice?* Take notes and put them in the drawer. *How can I better keep the students focused on the task at hand?* Take notes and put them in the drawer. *How can I make this classroom look like a precision prototypical environment of classroom learning and student management during the principal's scheduled observations?* Take notes and put them in the drawer. This practice continued for forty-one years. It was a practice that yielded some very positive and productive outcomes, or my career would not have lasted as long as it did. Once again, I had a feeling of accomplishment, as if I had achieved a mastery of something, only this time it was how to structure and direct a high-functioning classroom. Like so many people who spend decades in their chosen field, I knew that I had accumulated a substantial amount of knowledge that was experience based. The thought occurred to me that if I could pass on some of the more practical aspects of my forty-one years of knowledge to younger teachers, maybe they could take what I now know and use that as their starting point and expand professionally from there.

While attempting to conceptualize how I would like to share my accumulated storehouse of information, I took notice of several things. First, my practice of note-taking yielded not only some positive and productive outcomes once put into practice, but also a significant number of written notes. Second, the preponderance of curriculum in teacher education programs centers out of necessity on student safety, closing the achievement gap, school and classroom climate policies and practices, gender and racial equity efforts, common core standards, antibullying policies, various sociopolitical issues, and vogue trends that are transient in nature, consequently leaving the "nuts and bolts" aspect of structuring a classroom environment largely neglected. Third, this largely neglected aspect of the teaching profession has been delegated to cooperating teachers in student teaching programs and to school administrators during the teacher evaluation process to "backfill" as needed. For those who may not know, teachers and building administrators have multiple demands on every second of their time during their workday. Nearly all of these demands require a level of immediate attention that would place them as a higher priority than the time and detail necessary to assist a colleague in learning how to structure a productive parent conference for instance. Finally, as previously pointed out, near and dear to my heart is organization. Also, near and dear to my heart is a pragmatic approach to all tasks. So while connecting these points, the vision became clear. Create a book that is a practical nuts and bolts "field manual" that holds information that when utilized will create the structure necessary for a high-functioning classroom. I offer you this topical breakdown of ways to sequentially prepare for the events contained within a school year as an organizational tool for preservice teachers and those currently in the profession who are looking for ways to improve their planning and organizational skills. I hope the information contained within this quick reference manual proves effective for your students' learning and enhances the mastery of your teaching style.

Chapter 1

Establishing a Personal Philosophy of Instruction and Classroom Climate Policies

Every man is a creature of the age in which he lives, and few are able to raise themselves above the ideas of the time.

—Voltaire

WHY HAVE A PERSONAL PHILOSOPHY OF INSTRUCTION AND CLASSROOM CLIMATE POLICIES?

In any given endeavor it is important to have an established personal philosophy in place. It will serve as a collection of general principles that will provide guidance in making the specific litany of decisions that will be required of every person over the course of a career and a lifetime. Written policies that proceed from that philosophy should be in place as well. These policies will assist in transitioning the philosophy from principle into practice. Nowhere is this more apparent than in the dynamic atmosphere of a K–12 classroom. This is where the teacher has been assigned to lead a group of children, society's most precious assets and resources, on the pathway of developing everyone's unique intellectual abilities, all the while acting *in loco parentis,* legally in place of a parent, from doorstep to doorstep.

Given the responsibility placed upon classroom teachers, having a written personal and practical philosophy of instruction and accompanying classroom climate policy becomes a valuable tool for you that will serve many purposes, including, but not limited to, the following:

- A building block for effective job application materials and subsequent interviews.
- A building block for a clear and concise course outline and/or syllabus.
- A point of reference that will assist students, parents, and administrators in understanding the rationale for your classroom policies, especially on the student's first day of school and parent Back to School Night.
- A guideline when crafting and revising lesson plans and classroom rules.
- A reference tool for pre- and postobservation conferences with administration.

Even though the stakeholders mentioned above may hold a personal reservation on the finer points of a given philosophy of instruction and/or classroom climate policies, once they read a well-written, coherent, and logical copy they are much more likely to respect your judgment and cooperate with the direction that has been set.

WHAT IS AN EXAMPLE OF A PERSONAL PHILOSOPHY OF INSTRUCTION AND CLASSROOM CLIMATE?

There are as many ways in which a teacher may wish to craft this document as there are teachers. Feel free to create a personalized version but be concise and logical. Figure 1.1 contains an example utilized in actual practice. Along with a personal philosophy of instruction, I include additional components of attendance and late work policy; curriculum, instruction, and assessment; as well as student management policy for distribution to students, parents, and administration.

Figure 1.1 A Personal Philosophy of Instruction and Classroom Climate Policies

I. PHILOSOPHY OF INSTRUCTION

My personal philosophy of instruction is simply to provide the highest quality instruction possible and to teach each student with the same energy and resolve as if she or he were my own child. This level of instruction is characterized by

   a. A linear alignment of prescribed curriculum, instructional best practices, and accurate assessment for the purpose of informing future group and individual instruction and remediation.
   b. Pedagogical strategies that are age appropriate and represent best instructional practices.
   c. An emphasis placed on both direct instruction and student-centered class activities with each student taking a participatory role in all class proceedings.
   d. An emphasis on individual research, writing, and presentation skills.
   e. Maximum time efficiency inside and outside of class.
   f. Systematic procedure, structure, and organization.

II. ATTENDANCE AND LATE WORK POLICY

Unless otherwise directed by district and school policy, my attendance and late work policy is as follows:

   a. Daily student attendance is required and necessary for the successful completion of this course.
   b. All assignments must be turned in by the end of the class period in which they are due.
   c. Based on one day's grace period for each day of an excused absence, makeup work will be accepted for full credit.
   d. Late work will be accepted for a maximum of 50 percent of an assignment's value.

(continued)

Figure 1.1 *(continued)*

III. CURRICULUM, INSTRUCTION, AND ASSESSMENT

a. Curriculum—Course curriculum will be planned in accordance with established state and district guidelines.
b. Instruction—Instruction will range from direct forms of instruction to various models of student-centered activities as instructionally appropriate.
c. Assessment—All graded assignments will be given with maximum advance notice and with clearly delineated assessment criteria. Assessment will be done on a points and percentage basis. The grading breakdown will be as follows:

$$100–90\% = A$$
$$89–80\% = B$$
$$79–70\% = C$$
$$69–60\% = D$$
$$59–00\% = F$$

IV. CLASSROOM CLIMATE POLICY

The classroom climate policy will coincide with the policies set forth in the district handbook regarding student responsibilities, rights, and discipline. The application of this handbook will be characterized by the following:

a. In the unlikely event that any student management issues should arise, the philosophical approach used will be correction-based rather than punitive.
b. Each student and the teacher will always recognize and respect the rights of all other individuals to physical safety and mental well-being.
c. Each student will respect district and personal property at all times.

d. Each student will recognize and respect the rights of all students to learn and for all teachers to always instruct in an appropriate learning environment.
e. Each student will recognize and respect the school district as an alcohol, drug, and weapon free environment always.

FINAL THOUGHTS REGARDING A PHILOSOPHY OF INSTRUCTION AND CLASSROOM CLIMATE POLICIES

Teachers must remember to keep their writing professional, sequenced, logical, and concise. A balance between a superior work ethic and consideration for making tasks manageable for their students and themselves should be implied in their writing. Throughout the process of developing an overall philosophy and policies, you should internally plan for student stress and self-stress management as it may arise. Finally, always remember the basics of instruction and classroom climate. All teachers will see a series of educational trends introduced into the profession during a career with many touted as a final pedagogical panacea; these trends will come and go, but the rudiments of good teaching last forever. Keep in mind that a quality philosophy of instruction and established classroom climate policies will lead to many

Figure 1.2 The Residual Benefits of a Quality Philosophy of Instruction and Classroom Climate Policies

Quality Philosophy of Instruction and
Classroom Climate Policies
|
Clear Understanding by Students, Parents, and Administrators
|
Quality Lesson Plans and Learning Environment
|
Successful Annual Evaluations

residual benefits, such as a clear understanding by students, parents, and administrators of classroom events; quality lesson plans and a quality learning environment; quality teaching and learning experiences; and a successful annual teaching evaluation. Please refer to figure 1.2.

QUESTIONS AND PRACTICES FOR CRITICAL THOUGHT

1. Define the term *philosophy* in your own words.
2. Research and summarize three examples of philosophies held by high profile professionals from fields outside of education.
3. Hypothetically place yourself in an interview for a teaching position. The principal or a committee member asks you to give a brief statement describing your philosophy of instruction. How would you respond?
4. Hypothetically place yourself in a parent–teacher conference; the parent spontaneously asks you to describe your "classroom discipline" philosophy. How would you respond?
5. Do you believe that there is a correspondent relationship between a quality philosophy of instruction and a quality classroom climate philosophy/policy, or do you view them as discrete components present in the classroom dynamic? Explain your reasoning.
6. A categorical imperative can be loosely explained as an unconditional moral obligation that is binding in all circumstances. List and explain any personal moral imperatives that you would incorporate into your array of educational philosophies.
7. This chapter opens with a quote from the French Enlightenment writer Francois-Marie Arouet, commonly known as Voltaire, "Every man is a creature of the age in which he lives, and few are able to raise themselves above the ideas of the time." List and explain what you consider to be the ideas of our time as it relates to K–12 education. Separate these ideas into two subjective categories of "sound ideas" and "unsound ideas." Further explain how we might collectively or individually rise above unsound ideas relating to K–12 education.

8. John Dewey, among his many academic roles, served as an educational reformer during the late nineteenth and twentieth centuries. He believed that first and foremost a child's education is a social experience and not a job preparation experience. Do you agree or disagree with John Dewey on this point? Provide rationale for your reasoning.
9. Jean Piaget, B. F. Skinner, Benjamin Bloom, and Howard Gardner are all prominent educational theorists and philosophers of the twentieth century. Compare and contrast the ideas of these four people.
10. Maria Montessori was a prominent Italian physician and educational philosopher of the late nineteenth and early twentieth centuries. Montessori put forward as a basis of argument that students learn best under the conditions of independent and self-directed learning that is conducted in a self-paced manner. In your opinion, would this approach be successful in the classrooms of the twenty-first century? Provide rationale for your assessment.

DEVELOPMENT ACTIVITY NUMBER 1

Create a formal, written, and custom philosophy of instruction and classroom climate policies that are age appropriate for the level you teach or hope to teach. Remember to incorporate the principles suggested in this chapter.

Chapter 2

Understanding Your Community and Student Population

Any fool can know. The point is to understand.

—Albert Einstein

WHY IS IT IMPORTANT TO UNDERSTAND YOUR COMMUNITY?

This is a key question because when a teacher understands the varied characteristics that may exist within a given community, it allows for enhanced proactive planning in the multiple decision-making processes teachers are responsible for throughout the school year. More specifically:

- It creates a heightened teacher sensitivity to the cultural differences that may exist within the community they serve.
- It creates a heightened awareness in teachers of the unique circumstances of, and resulting needs within, the community that they serve.
- It may narrow the spectrum of anticipated contexts that teachers must prepare for when planning communication with parents.

Serving as a very current and relevant example, many school districts—especially in urban areas compared with their suburban counterparts—often struggle greatly with ongoing efforts to close the achievement gap. Teaching in contrasting environments such as urban versus rural, private versus public, progressive versus conservative, may inherently pose disparate circumstances in terms of sociological considerations within the teaching-learning processes.

At this point, consider three additional points of caution: First, as a teacher, you should not make any assumptions about individual or family priorities or direction. Although you may work in a high school that sends 95 percent of its graduates directly into the workforce, it does not mean that an individual student or family does not place a premium on opportunities in higher education. Second, regardless of your best intention, you should not attempt to "override" community beliefs to adjust them to be more in line with your own personal societal beliefs. Finally, and most important, under no circumstance should you ever use demographic data in a manner that establishes any new, or reinforces any previously existing, biases.

WHY IS IT IMPORTANT TO UNDERSTAND YOUR STUDENT POPULATION?

You should understand your student population for the initial purpose of gaining a clear view of each student's academic history. This is the best way to inform not only strategies for the aggregate academic success of a group of students, but especially the strategies for each individual student's academic success. This type of information is best gained by the taking the following steps:

- Talking to each student's teachers from previous years and classes.
- Obtaining a general familiarity of each student's cumulative folders in advance of the start of the school year.

These cumulative folders are highly confidential and contain, among other things, school and registration/transfer records, attendance records, report cards, standardized test scores, individual school photos, and possible special educational accommodations that have been accumulated over the years. When examining an individual student's cumulative folder, the following focal points may be most helpful to you:

- Transcripts of grades to reveal any consistent patterns.
- Results of standardized tests scores from year to year. This may show patterns and reveal any academic strengths that need to be built on and/or any academic weaknesses that need to be remediated. It must be pointed out that it is quite common for report card results and standardized test scores to be asynchronous.
- Any individual special education plans such as individualized education plans (IEPs) and 504 plans. IEPs are written plans for students who qualify for special educational services. These plans ensure that students with disabilities receive a free and appropriate public education in the least restrictive environment. Similarly, 504 plans are crafted for students who do not meet the criteria for special education services but are still in need of accommodations for academic success.
- All accommodations that the student may have received. Such accommodations are subject to annual revision but do carry over from academic year to academic year and remain in effect until their terminal point, at which parents sign off on the documents.

Again, you'll want to guard against making any preconceived judgments about any given student from the information contained in their cumulative folders. In a positive direction, students grow physically, intellectually, and emotionally from year to year so that what might have held true in fifth grade may not hold true in sixth grade. Further, students quite often respond to different teachers in different ways due to the subject matter and/or styles of instruction offered to them, so student performance may shift sharply upward with a new school year. On the other hand, a significant drop in student performance may indicate exogenous environmental change(s) that are negatively affecting physical or emotional health. In the latter case, speaking with the student's counselor and/or administration will be the professionally responsible course of action.

WHAT COMMON LOGICAL FALLACIES EXIST IN THE PK–12 ENVIRONMENT?

A logical fallacy is simply an argument forwarded by an individual that appears to be reasonable on the surface but is invalidated after it fails the test of reason. If you become familiar with some of these most common logical fallacies, you will see them on many occasions, even in the K–12 school environment:

1. The ad hominem fallacy (attacking the person's character rather than their reasoning on an issue).

"I don't care if the graduation rate has increased 20 percent at the local high school, Principal Jones is nothing more than a slick-talking people pleaser."

2. The post hoc fallacy (event A occurred before event B; therefore, event A must have caused event B to happen).

"Since Miss Jones has been the English Department chairperson standardized test scores have increased for each student enrolled in an English class. She is doing excellent work raising test scores."

3. The appeal to common belief fallacy (everybody believes that X is true so it must be true).

"Everyone I have talked to just loves the new mathematics curriculum so it must be good."

4. The red herring fallacy (person A posits position X, person B diverts the topic by putting forward position Y).

Dad 1: "Coach Hammer sure is an offensive football genius and the team is undefeated."

Dad 2: "Yeah, but Coach Hammer doesn't have the people skills that Coach Bennett did last season."

One of the most common logical fallacies present in the K–12 environment is the fallacy of composition (what is true for the part is also true for the whole). When it comes to a teacher understanding their community and student populations, they must take special care to avoid this error of generalization. Can you think of potential examples of the fallacy of composition being present in the thinking of a classroom teacher?

"If only I knew then what I know now."
—Said everyone at one time or another.

FINAL THOUGHTS REGARDING UNDERSTANDING YOUR COMMUNITY AND STUDENT POPULATION

The stated topic of this chapter merits an important corollary: not only is it necessary to know and understand the characteristics of the community in which you work and the abilities of your students, you must also know yourself and your compatibility with the sociopolitical ethos of a given community. If such compatibility is not present, then you must sincerely assess your abilities to adapt. Earlier in this chapter I advised not to attempt to "override" community beliefs to adjust them to be more in line with your own societal beliefs. Therefore, it is important for you to take this corollary into account during the application process.

QUESTIONS AND PRACTICES FOR CRITICAL THOUGHT

1. In your own words, define *cultural differences*. List and explain an array of potential cultural differences that may exist in each community. Further explain how these cultural differences may affect a given school building or classroom dynamic.
2. In your own words, define *achievement gap*. What do you believe to be the causes of the achievement gap? In your opinion, what steps should be taken by the educational establishment to close this gap?

3. List and explain common assumptions about individual or family priorities or direction that a teacher may make. Explain how these assumptions, especially unconscious assumptions, can be guarded against through the process of introspection.
4. Explain why it would be considered ill-advised for a teacher to attempt to "override" community beliefs in an effort to adjust them to be more in line with their own societal beliefs.
5. Consider the community in which you received your own K–12 education. List what you believe to have been some varied community characteristics that may have had some bearing on your district's or your school's educational direction.
6. List and explain what you think may be common community characteristics that educators might factor in when making policy decisions. Explain the criteria that you think should be applied when distinguishing between community characteristics that are truly relevant or those characteristics that are merely superfluous to the educational process.
7. List at least three commonly identifiable community characteristics that you would consider to be highly relevant to informing your approach to instruction, classroom management, and parent–teacher interaction. Further, isolate at least one of these characteristics and explain in detail how you would strategically integrate that information into your teaching methods.
8. Describe what information you might find in each student's cumulative folder. What approach should a professional educator take as he or she begins to interpret the information contained within. Further, explain why the cumulative folders are considered highly confidential.
9. Describe several ways in which you might parlay cumulative folder content, in part or in whole, into academic success for a given student.
10. Hypothetically place yourself in an interview for a teaching position. The principal or a committee member presents you with the following scenario: "One of your students consistently scores above the 90th percentile on a national standardized test of academic skills across multiple subject matters over the years. Yet this student has a long-running pattern of subaverage class grades on report cards for the same range of subject

matters. What instructional/motivational strategy or strategies would you employ to assist this student in moving her or his class grades upward to be more in line with their standardized test scores?" How would you respond?
11. Research the difference between logical fallacies and cognitive biases. Explain how these errors in thought ingress into educator performance, how to detect them, and how they can be adjusted for.

DEVELOPMENT ACTIVITY NUMBER 2

One of the best sources of relevant information about communities can be found, arranged by zip code, on the website provided by the US Census Bureau. Go to https://www.census.gov/quickfacts/fact/table/US/PST045219 and access the community that you teach in, or hope to teach in, and learn more about that community.

Chapter 3

Preparing a Classroom for a New Academic Year

By failing to prepare, you are preparing to fail.

—Benjamin Franklin

WHAT ARE THE STEPS TO TAKE IN PREPARING A CLASSROOM FOR A NEW ACADEMIC YEAR?

When a new school year approaches teachers will no doubt receive a very cordial welcome letter from the principal. This letter and the accompanying documents will be replete with all kinds of information, not the least of which is a reminder of the start date of the teacher work year. They will also see attached a schedule of activities that are planned for the faculty and staff for the coming teacher in-service week, or "zero week," as it is sometimes called. There will probably be a time scheduled for activities like new teacher orientation, general faculty meetings, department or grade level meetings, technology update trainings, updates on lunchtime procedures, first aid and CPR training, new curriculum trainings, professional development in the form of informational meetings or trainings on various matters that the district deems priorities for the upcoming school year, child safety training (preventing and reporting child abuse), and review of new and existing IEP and/or 504 content in consultation with the counselors, just to name a few.

What teachers will probably not see is a schedule providing adequate time to properly prepare their classroom for the first day of school.

If you are ever faced with this initial complication of the school year, you will have two choices in front of you. How you make your selection depends on your personal threshold for stress and/or personal penchant for general efficiency.

Option One—Wait to show up for work on the Monday of which in-service week begins and spend most or all of your days in meetings, mentally multitasking though said meetings, forfeiting lunchtime in favor of task completion, then working into the night and over the next couple of weekends preparing your classroom for the first day of school.

Option Two—Show up on the Monday one week before in-service week begins so as to devote your time, thoughts, and efforts directly and solely to the purpose of leisurely preparing the classroom just the way you envision it for the first day of school. Then you have the freedom of paying attention during a week of meetings, having adequate time for lunch, checking in with colleagues, leaving the building and the daily concerns behind in the late afternoon, enjoying your evenings and upcoming weekends, and enjoying family and/or personal interests.

Even though it means working an uncompensated extra week, most teachers will find it is more than worth it to select the option of coming in a week early to prepare their classrooms entirely, insofar as possible, for the first day of school prior to in-service week. The rationale for this choice is directed by the following considerations: (1) Stress levels will be greatly reduced during in-service week, during the ensuing evenings, and over weekends when one's classroom is fully set up and ready for students on the first day of school. (2) All students always deserve their teacher's best performance, and that best performance will not occur when splitting one's mental energy between meeting content and classroom preparation. (3) Divided attention is the portal to error and errors often arrive in the form of omissions in organization. Be assured that any lapse in organization on the part of a teacher, no matter how small, is always noticed by the students and often acted upon in some manner. Suffice it to say that students have somewhat of a "zero tolerance policy" for any semblance of lack of planning and/or organization on the part of a teacher.

Preparing a Classroom for a New Academic Year

WHAT ARE THE SPECIFIC ORGANIZATIONAL STEPS TO TAKE TWO WEEKS BEFORE STUDENTS ARRIVE?

Refer to figure 3.1 as a checklist of recommended tasks to be completed two weeks prior to the arrival of students to help ensure a timely, organized, and stress-free start to your school year.

Figure 3.1 Checklist of Organizational Steps to Take Two Weeks before Students Arrive

Date Completed:

1. _____Create a logbook of tasks completed for each month. This is especially important when beginning a new position. This allows for an easy reference in the future for tasks that must be completed on a month-by-month basis.
2. _____Arrange your desk in an optimal location taking into consideration computer location, proximity to the classroom intercom, teacher vantage point for general student classroom supervision, teacher vantage point for outside activities that one is not directly responsible for, including other class recesses, outside activities such as unauthorized person(s) on school grounds, and so on.
3. _____Arrange the student desks in an optimal formation taking into consideration formal and informal interaction among the students, nature of the upcoming class activities, position of the projection screen for student viewing, etc.
4. _____Sanitize all desks, surfaces, and doorknobs.
5. _____Place a "nose blowing station" complete with tissues, garbage can, and hand sanitizers at the farthest point possible from student desks and your desk.
6. _____Arrange and organize a classroom book library if possible.

(continued)

Figure 3.1 *(continued)*

7. _____Obtain a copy of the academic master calendar for the school year as determined by your building administration and/or school district.
8. _____Purchase a personal academic-year calendar planning book arranged by the months of the school year, either in electronic form or in hardcover.
9. _____Secure copies of the national content standards to be used in the subject matter and/or grade level to be taught.
10. _____Secure copies of the state content standards to be used in the subject matter and or grade level to be taught.
11. _____Secure copies of the district content standards to be used in the subject matter and/or grade level to be taught.
12. _____Secure copies of the student textbooks to be used, teacher's editions of those textbooks, and any of the publisher's supplemental materials such as teacher's manuals, test banks, lab activities, and accompanying workbooks/reproducible materials.
13. _____Prepare a course outline/syllabus based on content standards and the selected textbooks for distribution to students, parents, and administrators.
14. _____Prepare a personal classroom audio/visual library or list of appropriate and relevant online resources to support instruction.
15. _____Prepare classroom and/or hallway bulletin boards.
16. _____Purchase an old-fashioned teacher's lesson planning book, use it, and leave it on your desk in plain sight every night upon leaving the building. Not only will this planning book provide any substitute teacher information about what to do for the day, especially when an unplanned or emergency absence should occur on your part, it will also allow you to informally sketch out future lesson plans and ideas.

17. _____ Create a professional development unit (PDU) logbook and use it. Because most or all states require teachers to complete a set number of professional development hours at regular intervals for license renewal, it is beneficial to record every teacher education class, training, in-service, and such that you are present for in a logbook. It eliminates the need to rely solely on memory when submitting a listing of your PDUs to the state when applying for license renewal. You might find many of the activities of teacher in-service week helpful in meeting the state's professional development requirements. Remember to keep all completion certificates in a safe place for they may be required to validate your attendance and completion of the sessions.
18. _____ Gather the materials for each student to prepare a personal work sample file. I highly recommend that every teacher keeps a work sample file for each student; this will serve several purposes, not the least important coming at parent conferences. This would be a good time to obtain these files and place blank labels for student names on each. The students will enjoy personalizing these work sample files by decorating their exterior during a future class session. This will be addressed in detail in a later chapter.
19. _____ Create a model student portfolio to share with the students. I also highly recommend that each student keeps a personal portfolio in the form of an accordion file, binder, or one of the many other forms of organizing papers for the current grading period. The purpose of these portfolios is to serve as a bank of receipts, so to speak, for papers that you have graded, recorded, and returned to each student. This is invaluable when the gradebook is not showing a score for a particular assignment for a given student. One of the most common statements that all teachers hear is a student declaring, "Why is that assignment missing? I turned that in to you!" The teacher then can respond with, "If you did indeed submit that assignment to me then I would have graded it and returned it to you. Please

(continued)

Figure 3.1 *(continued)*

> check your portfolio." If the student cannot produce the assignment in question from her or his portfolio, then the omission simply belongs to the student. If the student can produce the completed, graded, and returned assignment, then the omission belongs to the teacher and an admission of error and apology is in order. This is important for the purpose of modeling humility and ownership of mistakes. You might also find it helpful in the case of a missing assignment to check the student's attendance for the day the assignment in question was due. If the student was absent the day it was due, that may help solve the mystery.
>
> 20. _____Gather all desk supplies such as pencils, pens, scissors, and markers.
> 21. _____If possible, complete all photocopying of the first two weeks of student materials such as course outlines, syllabi, packets, lab forms, study guides, current event templates, research paper guidelines, quizzes, examinations, etc. Below you will find a checklist of recommended tasks to be completed one week prior to the arrival of students to help ensure a timely, organized, and stress-free start to the school year.

WHAT ARE THE SPECIFIC ORGANIZATIONAL STEPS TO TAKE ONE WEEK BEFORE STUDENTS ARRIVE?

Refer to figure 3.2 as a checklist of recommended tasks to complete and items to gather during in-service week, one week before the students arrive.

Figure 3.2 Checklist of Organizational Steps to Take One Week before Students Arrive

Date Completed:

1. _____Attend all scheduled meetings and record in detail all professional development units earned.
2. _____Create a class book (a binder) that includes, but is not limited to, the following items: a personal planning calendar book, a lesson plan book, a copy of your teaching schedule, class seating charts, room use assignments, various bell schedules, school master calendar, emergency procedures especially for evacuation and lockdown drills, class lists, school intercom directory, locker combinations, student computer user names/passwords, "no photo" lists of students as requested by the parents, parent contact information for both email and phone numbers work/home/cell, parent contact log, medical conditions, where medications are located, IEPs, 504s, and any other student information. In the event of any emergency evacuation, take this book with you!
3. _____Transfer all information from the school's/district's master calendar to the dates in your personal planning calendar. Be certain to pencil in any school- or district-wide events that may override established instructional plans such as assemblies, late openings, early dismissals, scheduled holidays, teacher in-service days, beginning and end of semesters, and so on. This information will significantly preclude many frustrations regarding teaching efforts to complete all curricular requirements. Further, include any academic/communication/evaluation tasks for each day as well as any scheduled supervision duties, faculty meetings, parent conferences, and other such responsibilities.
4. _____Obtain and read all employee information such as the master contract between teachers and the district, employee handbook, and building faculty handbook.

(continued)

Figure 3.2 *(continued)*

5. _____Obtain all of your personal computer login information and check that the school assigned computer, projector, sound system, and printer are ready for immediate instructional use. Seek assistance from your building or district IT specialist as needed.
6. _____Create and review the system for locker assignments to include preparation to patiently assist those students who may need a review of how to open a combination lock.
7. _____Develop and document plans for a class service project if required.
8. _____Create an end of the day class dismissal book if your required duty includes supervising a pickup car line. The main office should provide a list of parent-approved names of persons who are cleared to collect and drive each child home. I highly recommend that you place each of these pages in a plastic cover sheet to preserve them during wet weather.
9. _____Complete any forms that the main office should require. This may include your personal emergency information, personal biography for the school website, etc.
10. _____Complete and submit any work order request to building maintenance for any broken and/or unsafe conditions in your assigned classroom, building, and grounds.
11. _____Become familiar with the attendance/lunch count/dismissal procedures.
12. _____Prepare any annual written goals to be submitted to the building principal for the annual teacher evaluation process.
13. _____Begin planning for the month of September.

Preparing a Classroom for a New Academic Year 25

WHAT WILL NEED TO BE PLANNED AND PREPARED FOR DURING THE MONTH OF SEPTEMBER?

With the school year under way, you will find yourself quite engaged with student contact time, lesson planning, paper grading, and administrative tasks, as well as with a variety of regularly scheduled meetings. You will now be aware of how valuable task completion has been from the prior two weeks' checklists. At any rate, there will be some specific tasks that September requires. Figure 3.3 shows a partial checklist of recommended tasks.

Figure 3.3 Checklist of the Organizational Steps to Take during the Month of September

Date Completed:

1. _____Plan and prepare for Back to School Night for parents. For the upper grades it is recommended that you provide each set of parents with a copy of the course outline for your class and review it with them. Primarily the parents are interested in what their child will be learning, the general approach to instruction, and most important, how assignments and their requirements such as due dates will be communicated, as well as how their child will be graded on those assignments. Again, with the upper grades a teacher may have only three to six minutes per class to communicate all relevant information.
2. _____Plan and prepare for a school-wide Jog-a-Thon.
3. _____Plan and prepare for school picture day.
4. _____Plan and prepare for school picture retake day.
5. _____Plan and prepare for high school/college visitation and/or shadow days.
6. _____Plan and prepare for student body election speeches and voting.

(continued)

Figure 3.3 (continued)

7. _____ Plan and prepare for any assemblies that are or are not scheduled.
8. _____ Plan and prepare for a meeting with room parents when applicable.
9. _____ Begin planning the month of October.

WHAT WILL NEED TO BE PLANNED AND PREPARED FOR DURING THE MONTH OF OCTOBER?

Figure 3.4 Checklist of the Organizational Steps to Take during the Month of October

Date Completed:

1. _____ Plan for a statewide teacher in-service day if applicable. This is a good day to obtain relevant and documentable professional development units.
2. _____ Begin discussions and additional paperwork as required by the building principal regarding the annual teacher evaluation process.
3. _____ Prepare for any Halloween assemblies or room parties if applicable.
4. _____ Begin planning the month of November.

WHAT WILL NEED TO BE PLANNED AND PREPARED FOR DURING THE MONTH OF NOVEMBER?

Figure 3.5 Checklist of the Organizational Steps to Take during the Month of November

Date Completed:

1. _____Be aware of the many dates in November on which instruction will be preempted, such as Veteran's Day, Thanksgiving, etc.
2. _____Plan for an end-of-quarter grading process. Taper class instruction to coincide with the natural break point at the end of the grading period and before issuing grades.
3. _____Prepare for parent–teacher conferences. This topic will be addressed in detail in an upcoming chapter.
4. _____Prepare for a school-wide book fair if applicable.
5. _____Begin planning the month of December.

WHAT WILL NEED TO BE PLANNED AND PREPARED FOR DURING THE MONTH OF DECEMBER?

Figure 3.6 Checklist of the Organizational Steps to Take during the Month of December

Date Completed:

1. _____ Plan and prepare for classroom observations by your building administrator.
2. _____ Be aware of any dates that will accommodate holiday activities in terms of assemblies, evening programs, etc.
3. _____ Beginning planning the month of January.
4. _____ Enjoy your winter break.

WHAT WILL NEED TO BE PLANNED AND PREPARED FOR DURING THE MONTHS OF JANUARY THROUGH JUNE?

Figure 3.7 Checklist of the Organizational Steps to Take during the Months of January through June

Date Completed:

1. _____Plan according to the school and district calendar, keeping a keen eye on holidays, spring vacation days, end of quarter dates, end of semester/trimester dates, dates for final examinations, deadlines for submission of grades, updating cumulative folders, and so on.
2. _____In common practice, the building administration will provide a checklist of items to be completed by teachers before they depart at the end of the school year. The more careful attention paid to the items on the checklist the easier it will be to transition into the coming school year.

FINAL THOUGHTS ON PREPARING A CLASSROOM FOR A NEW ACADEMIC YEAR

There is a sequence to putting a plan into place. An idea is conceived, a plan is made to put the idea into practice, the plan is implemented, the results are evaluated, and finally any needed adjustments are made. At the core of this sequence are the steps of "think, plan, do." Many times, young adolescents possess a prefrontal cortex that has not reached full development. Consequently, some of their actions are impulsive, consisting of only the "do" step without the "think and plan" steps preceding the action. As professional educators we must always be mindful of the "think, plan, do" sequence in our own approach to classroom operations. The more we apply ourselves to the thinking and planning stages, the more successful the implementation phase will become for teacher and student.

QUESTIONS AND PRACTICES
FOR CRITICAL THOUGHT

1. In the form of a schematic diagram, create a timeline for planning an academic year.
2. Explain why advanced planning is essential in every profession.
3. What is "zero week?" Explain why the week before zero week, zero week, and week one can have a profound effect on the month of September, and possibly the span of the school year, for a given classroom.
4. Explain the purpose of keeping a logbook. List and explain the benefits of keeping a logbook throughout the school year. Further, list and explain how a logbook replete with notations could positively affect the planning process in subsequent school years.
5. Compile a listing of typical district- and school-wide events that classroom instruction must be planned around. Explain methods teachers can employ to create a smooth coexistence between these two important elements of a child's educational experience.
6. Compose a listing of common questions that you would anticipate parents will want the answers to during a presentation on Back to School Night. Create a comprehensive prototype Back to School Night presentation for parents that incorporates these answers with all other relevant information you wish to convey.
7. Cite several reasons why students keeping a portfolio containing all graded and returned work is beneficial to both the students and their teachers.
8. Some building principals require that each teacher submit detailed weekly lesson plans before 8:00 a.m. every Monday morning, often in a prescribed format, and some principals may even offer a written critique. Some building principals do not require written lesson plans except in the event of a teacher needing a substitute teacher. From a classroom teacher's perspective, list and explain the pros and cons of each of these administrative practices.
9. Hypothetically place yourself in an interview for a teaching position. The principal or a committee member presents you

with the following scenario: "You have prepared an in-depth PowerPoint presentation for your students that represents a great deal of effort on your part and of which you are particularly proud to present. Unfortunately, upon beginning your presentation, the classroom projection device suddenly becomes completely inoperable requiring the attention of an IT specialist. Describe your Plan B.
10. In your opinion, is it preferable to complete your planning efforts by creating detailed written plans or by just keeping your plans mentally cataloged for the sake of expediency? Provide rationale for your choice.

DEVELOPMENT ACTIVITY NUMBER 3

Create a logbook of tasks completed for each month. Again, this is especially important when beginning new employment or any new position. Begin by entering any tasks that you have completed in chronological order.

Chapter 4

Knowing the Curriculum and What Is Expected of You

> Discipline is knowing what to do. Knowing when to do it. Doing it to the best of your abilities. Doing it that way every single time.
>
> —Coach Bobby Knight

Traditionally, the general educational process has been centered around three successive processes: curriculum, instruction, and evaluation—the latter also sometimes referred to as measurement or assessment. We must be clear on two points regarding these three processes. First, all three of these must align. In other words, what is measured in terms of student learning is actually based on the specific content taught, which was the actual content prescribed. Second, even though these three processes must share a linear alignment, the responsibilities for their creation, delivery, and assessment are out of necessity discrete, or individually separate and distinct, in terms of who is responsible for this creation, delivery, and assessment for the established results to be valid. So who is responsible for each component part?

WHO HAS RESPONSIBILITY FOR SETTING THE CURRICULUM?

Establishing the curriculum to be taught in all subject matters is the responsibility of the policymakers. More to the point, what is to be taught in the public K–12 environment is determined by local school boards, which must coincide with state boards of education requirements, which are directed by state legislatures and governors of each state. National associations such as the Council for Economic Education or the National Council of Teachers of English may make recommendations and attempt to influence the policymakers regarding subject matter content standards. However, since we live in a representative democracy, the power to determine curriculum remains firmly planted with the policymakers.

WHO HAS RESPONSIBILITY FOR INSTRUCTIONAL METHODS?

The responsibility for the delivery of instruction lies with the building principal (who is primarily designated as the school's instructional leader) and the classroom teachers. These are the people who hold one or more university degrees that firmly establish them as state licensed experts in human development and authorized experts in specific subject matter and pedagogy, which is the method and practice of teaching an academic subject or theoretical concept to children. Please take special note that there is no overlap in any direction between those responsible for creating curriculum and those responsible for the curriculum's delivery.

WHO HAS RESPONSIBILITY FOR EVALUATION, MEASUREMENT, AND ASSESSMENT?

The responsibility for measuring student learning outcomes is best placed with the entity closest to the prescribed curricula yet independent from local school districts. That would be each state's department of education. It must be clearly stated that the entire purpose of any standardized testing process is purely diagnostic in nature. When teachers possess accurate aggregate and individual student's achievement data, future instructional strategies will be properly informed to remediate identified weaknesses and build on identified strengths. Though national standardized testing services are excellent, a greater possibility exists for a disparate emphasis between the many local curricula and the single assessment instrument used to measure them. Some of the nation's largest school districts have in the past maintained their own in-house departments of testing and measurement. They have based this practice on the rationale that their district curriculum is unique and possibly more aligned to local student demographic considerations. This is a practice that is rarely, if ever, seen today and certainly open to the criticism that such a practice provides no basis for side-by-side state, regional, or national comparisons.

It is very important to add that teachers may find it quite valuable to implement the process of an in-class pretest, instruction, and posttest sequence. For example, prior to teaching a unit on the US Constitution, you might consider giving the students a pretest examination on general knowledge of the document (after thoroughly explaining to the students that this is only a diagnostic preinstruction test with no bearing on class grade), followed by teaching the unit, followed by a postinstruction test that does affect individual grades. Such a process would likely yield a significantly positive outcome regarding student learning relative to the Constitution. Not only would this provide valuable feedback for you, but also for the students, which might kindle the flame for future learning efforts.

FINAL THOUGHTS ON KNOWING THE CURRICULUM AND KNOWING WHAT IS EXPECTED OF YOU

Two points warrant repeating with special emphasis: (1) there must be a linear alignment between curriculum, instruction, and evaluation for the measurement of learning outcomes to be considered valid, and (2) there must be a total and inviolable separation of powers between the determination of what is to be taught, how it is to be taught, and how learning outcomes are to be measured. Nevertheless, we do not live in a perfect world. You should not be surprised to encounter attempts by stakeholders at lateral encroachment upon others' assigned authority as the rise and fall of the political temperature may occur. Given that district and school building personnel are closer to the parents and the local politically active community than a distant legislature or testing service, teachers may be the first to receive feedback from concerned adults.

QUESTIONS AND PRACTICES FOR CRITICAL THINKING

1. Create a simple schematic diagram breaking down the responsibilities for the adoption of curricula, the delivery of curricula, and the measurement of learning outcomes.
2. Explain what is meant by the statement, "There must be a linear alignment between curricula, instruction, and evaluation." List reasons why this linear alignment is imperative.
3. List existing factors that may create misalignments, or "offsets," between curricula, instruction, and measurement/evaluation of learning outcomes. List and explain the potential consequences that may occur from such curricular misalignments. Further, explain how these misalignments can be adjusted or corrected.
4. In your opinion, should there be a zone of curricular discretion available to classroom teachers? Explain your reasoning.
5. Because parents generally have no direct role in the selection of statewide curricula that is made available to local districts for implementation, no formal pedagogical training or direct role in instructional delivery, and no direct role in measuring learning outcomes, what role should parents assume in the educational processes that affect their children? Provide rationale for your position.
6. List some ways in which classroom teachers could develop and maintain a better understanding of parental frustrations or objections to required curricular components. Further list and explain ways in which teachers can professionally and effectively assist parents with these frustrations.
7. From a teacher's perspective, explain the value of an in-class pretest, instruction, and posttest sequence to larger learning outcomes.
8. Explain what is meant by these statements, "It must be clearly stated that the entire purpose of any standardized testing process is purely diagnostic in nature. When teachers possess accurate aggregate and individual student's achievement data, future instructional strategies will be properly informed to remediate identified weaknesses and build on identified strengths." Are you in agreement with these statements or do

you think the purpose of standardized testing and the resultant scores should go beyond diagnostic purposes to include rank ordering districts, schools, and teachers? Further, would you support the use of student standardized test scores as factors that help determine levels of district funding, teacher evaluation, and teacher pay? Provide rationale for your positions.
9. List and explain why national standardized tests and statewide standardized tests may yield disparate results.
10. Briefly research the process of disaggregating data from standardized test results. Explain how a teacher could use this information in future prescriptive teaching and learning processes.

DEVELOPMENT ACTIVITIES NUMBER 4

1. Locate, read, and understand all recommended national curriculum content standards for the subject matters and grade levels that you teach or plan to teach.
2. Locate, read, and understand all required state curriculum content standards prescribed by your state department of education through your state board of education for the subject matters and grade levels that you teach or plan to teach.
3. Locate, read, and understand all required local curriculum content standards for the subject matters and grade levels that you teach or plan to teach.
4. Locate, read, and understand the master bargaining labor agreement and terms and conditions of employment for your local school district.
5. Locate, read, and understand your building's teacher handbook.
6. Read and fully understand your job description.

Chapter 5

The First Steps of Planning Instruction

An ounce of prevention is worth a pound of cure.

—Benjamin Franklin

HOW IS THE PLANNING PROCESS STARTED?

As teachers, our prime objective is to maximize each student's cognitive potential. To the professional educator, the fulfillment of each student's potential is best quantified in the forms of subject matter mastery, critical thinking ability, utilization of problem-solving skills, creativity, and observable recognition of the need for responsible citizenship. Parents and students share in this vision of success; however, they may also place an additional, albeit often disproportionate, premium on standardized test scores, class grades, and being "engaged" in class. Consequently, parents and students may possibly assume the role of critical consumers of instructional strategies. To preclude the possibility of any dissonance regarding instructional strategies among the stakeholders of teacher, parents, and students, the crafting of masterful lesson plans merit significant time and effort on the teacher's part. Simply stated, there is nothing more important to the teaching and learning process than the daily lesson plan for each class session. There are additional reasons for this assertion. By creating your personalized effective delivery mechanism/system template, not only will you never have to craft lesson plans completely from scratch, but you will also accelerate the instructional planning process and economize planning time. Additionally, this will allow you to know exactly what will be happening in your classroom at any moment in time, reduce your general stress level, increase parental and administrative confidence in your performance thereby bolstering self-confidence, preclude or reduce off-task student behavior, and better engage students, leading to the maximization of learning outcomes quantified by any chosen metric.

WHAT ARE THE ESSENTIAL INSTRUCTIONAL TOOLS THAT MUST BE GATHERED BEFORE INSTRUCTION BEGINS?

As previously mentioned, the classroom teacher must begin by gathering some essential instructional tools. Refer to figure 5.1.

Figure 5.1 Checklist of the Essential Instructional Tools That Must Be Gathered before Instruction Begins

Date Completed:

1. _____All available subject matter standards documents, whether at the national, state, district, or building level, for all courses you are assigned to teach.
2. _____An annotated teacher edition textbook and all related supplement materials for each course you are assigned to teach.
3. _____A school and/or district instructional calendar for the year and a blank academic planning calendar.
4. _____A blank teacher's lesson plan book that includes week-by-week and day-by-day designated spaces for a quick view of the date, instructional topic, and main event of each daily class period. Commonly, these lesson plan books include spaces for bell schedules, instructions for substitute teachers, lunchtime duties, fire drill procedures,

nurse's office location, seating charts, and intercom numbers. It merits mention that this lesson plan book can mean the difference between a successful day or a miserable day for a substitute teacher, possibly for the building administrators and therefore for the regular teacher when they return to work. While it is best to leave detailed, really detailed, lesson plans for substitute teachers, we may not always be absent due to a planned event. In the case of an unplanned illness or family emergency, the sub can quickly reference the big picture of the day from this document. For a substitute teacher, only knowing that they should teach chapter 10, section 3, from the text on Thursday, January 14, is an entire world of difference from not knowing anything about what to do from 8:15 a.m. until 3:15 p.m.

5. _____A best practices tool kit for instruction should include three general, but essential, resources:
   a. A best practices model for the delivery of direct instruction. Examples of such are offered in chapter 8.
   b. A compendium of instruction models that will infuse lesson plans with a variety of pedagogical techniques that serve to reinforce your direct instruction efforts.
   c. A series of questioning strategies that serve to promote the development of critical thinking skills in students.

FINAL THOUGHTS CONCERNING THE FIRST STEPS OF PLANNING INSTRUCTION

The four phases of the planning sequence include the following:

1. Review the district and/or school calendar before the academic year begins and start to fill out all personal planning calendars noting all important dates.
2. Develop a long-term lesson plan for the academic year to include a course outline.
3. Plan weekly instruction.
4. Plan daily instruction.

An in-depth look at each of these phases will occur in the following chapters.

QUESTIONS AND PRACTICES FOR CRITICAL THOUGHT

1. In general, what are the advantages of planning any given activity? List and explain some of the advantages of detailed planning specific to classroom teachers.
2. List and explain the essential instructional tools necessary to begin the planning process. Are there any additional informational/organizational tools that you think helpful in the planning process other than those listed in the text? Provide rationale for your choices.
3. Research the phrase "best practices." In your own words, compose a definition of best practices.
4. Give at least three examples of teacher best practices that your research revealed. Would you add any best practices to the list that you believe would prove to be valid?
5. In your opinion, should best practices for teaching be research based to be considered valid for use in the classroom? Provide rationale for your position.
6. According to this author, what is the proper planning sequence? Are there additional steps that you would include in this sequence? Provide rationale for your choice.

DEVELOPMENT ACTIVITY NUMBER 5

Create three annotated bibliographies using the internet, libraries, or additional select sources. The first bibliography includes a listing of multiple resources for best practices of direct instruction. The second bibliography includes a listing of resources for models of various pedagogical techniques. The third bibliography includes a listing of resources for questioning strategies for use in a classroom setting. Include a written synopsis for each resource.

Chapter 6

Planning Instruction for a New Academic Year

Before anything else, preparation is the key to success.

—Alexander Graham Bell

HOW IS A YEARLONG LESSON PLAN DEVELOPED?

With copies of the school district's and/or school building's academic calendar for the coming year in hand, it is time for you to start the planning of instruction. You should begin by copying into your personal planning calendar all significant dates from the school year calendar to include the beginning of a term/semester, due dates for major projects, and midterm and final examinations to allow enough time to perform proper assessments. This will allow for the planning of instruction around school events that may preclude instruction on certain school days as well as school holidays. Refer to table 6.1.

Now that you know the overall curriculum, what is specifically expected from you, and all-important dates and events, it is time to begin breaking down the curriculum into three remaining parts for instructional purposes. First, develop a yearlong lesson plan that roughly spans from the first day of the school year until the last day of the school year. This yearlong plan includes a list of units by topic that may be further broken down into subtopics if you wish. Most likely

Table 6.1 Sample School Planning Calendar Week for the First Week of the School Year

September 5	September 6	September 7	September 8	September 9
Labor Day—NO SCHOOL	Welcome Assembly (Assembly Bell Schedule)	Begin Chapter 1 Instruction— Whole Numbers	Begin Preparation for Back to School Night	Assembly Schedule 9:30 Fire Safety Assembly— Fire Chief Guest Speaker
	Classroom Organization Day—Distribute Course Outline and Classroom Rules	3:30 Faculty Meeting	7:30 Grade Level Meeting	
	11:45 Cafeteria Duty		Begin Week 2 Planning in Blank Lesson Plan Book	Complete Weekly Lesson Plan for Week 2 and Post on Class Web Page
	Photocopy Materials for Week 2			

your principal will require this step as part of the teacher evaluation process. Second, from this yearlong lesson plan, weekly lesson plans can be developed. Third, and ultimately, the daily lesson plans that are now "laser focused," in a curricular sense, are in place for use directly with students. The latter two items are discussed in ensuing chapters.

As you begin developing a yearlong lesson plan, it is necessary to keep in mind that not all topics merit an exact equal amount of instruction time. For instance, if you are teaching a world literature class, the 83 pages and ensuing discussion regarding *The Analects of Confucius* will probably not demand as much time as the 731 pages and ensuing discussion regarding Homer's *Iliad* and *Odyssey*. Also, as the yearlong lesson plans expands, remember that there will be time constraints that will push against instruction due to the school year calendar and activities that displace instruction like assemblies. Of course, additional consideration must be given to the unexpected and inevitable fractures of continuous planned instruction due to unforeseen circumstances such as weather issues, emergency drills, and spontaneous assemblies when internal school issues arise. So it will be helpful to keep some type of informal contingency plan for the contraction of instruction as needed.

Let us assume for a moment that the state and aligned local school district content standards (which may vary based on locality) require in part or whole that each student at the middle and/or high school level learn about the structure and function of American government through the lens of the US Constitution. An example of a semester-long lesson plan format for a middle school or high school government/civics class might look like what is displayed in figure 6.1. The lesson plan is broken down into theoretical foundations, the Constitution, and American politics.

Figure 6.1 A Semester Lesson Plan for American Government

Weeks 1–5	UNIT I	Political Theory
	Week 1	John Locke
	Week 2	Jean Jacques Rousseau
	Week 3	Thomas Paine
	Week 4	Alexander Hamilton and Thomas Jefferson
	Week 5	The Federalist Papers
Weeks 6–12	UNIT II	The United States Constitution
	Week 6	The United States Constitution: Supreme Law of the Land
	Week 7	Article I: The Legislative Branch
	Week 8	Article II: The Executive Branch
	Week 9	Article III: The Judicial Branch
	Week 10	Articles IV through VII
	Week 11	The Bill of Rights: Amendments 1–10
	Week 12	Amendments 11–27
Weeks 13–18	UNIT III	American Politics
	Week 13	The Democratic Party Platform
	Week 14	The Republican Party Platform
	Week 15	Third Party Platforms
	Week 16	The Media and American Politics
	Week 17	Elections and Voting
	Week 18	Final Examination Week

Another example of a yearlong format for a middle or high school English composition and literature class whose content aligns with state and local school board direction—emphasis placed on state and local school board preapproval—might include the content as shown in figure 6.2. The course plan is divided into writing, American literature (both short stories and novels), world literature, and classic horror novels.

Figure 6.2 A Yearlong Lesson Plan for an English Composition and Literature Class

UNIT I	WRITING SKILLS	
	Week 1	Forms of Writing Expression
	Week 2	Free Writing
	Week 3	Narrative Writing
	Week 4	Descriptive Writing
	Week 5	Expository Writing
	Week 6	Persuasive Writing
	Week 7	Compare and Contrast
	Week 8	Reflective Writing
	Week 9	Writing Oral Histories
	Week 10	Biographical Writing
	Week 11	Writing Fiction
	Week 12	Writing Poetry
	Week 13	Writing Humor
UNIT II	AMERICAN LITERATURE—SHORT STORIES	
	Week 14	Washington Irving
	Week 15	Nathaniel Hawthorne
	Week 16	Edgar Allan Poe
	Week 17	Herman Melville
	Week 18	Semester Final Examination
	Week 19	Louisa May Alcott
	Week 20	Jack London
UNIT III	AMERICAN LITERATURE—NOVELS	
	Week 21	*The Adventures of Tom Sawyer*
	Week 22	*The Adventures of Huckleberry Finn*

	Week 23	*A Connecticut Yankee in King Arthur's Court*
	Week 24	*The Gilded Age*
	Week 25	*Malcom X*
	Week 26	*The Autobiography of Miss Jane Pittman*
	Week 27	*Bury My Heart at Wounded Knee*
	Week 28	*The Call of the Wild*
	Week 29	*The Catcher in the Rye*
UNIT IV	WORLD LITERATURE	
	Week 30	*The Works of William Shakespeare*
	Week 31	*The Works of Alexandre Dumas*
	Week 32	*Greek Mythology Week*
UNIT V	CLASSIC HORROR NOVELS	
	Week 33	*Dracula*
	Week 34	*Frankenstein*
	Week 35	*The Phantom of the Opera*
	Week 36	Semester Final Examination

HOW IS A COURSE OUTLINE DEVELOPED?

At this point you are ready to develop a high-quality course outline for distribution to students, parents, and administrators. In crafting course outlines, you should at least include course title, course description, content to be covered and a timeline, alignment to relevant content standards, assignment types, grading systems, provisions for academic assistance, provisions for opportunities for further challenge, contact information, and so on. This will become the governing document, so to speak, for your class that will bind both you and your students to its content. Please notice the content as shown in figure 6.3 that serves as an example of an actual course outline used in a semester-long Advanced Placement Microeconomics class at the high school level. Notice the Opportunities for Further Challenge element. Some states require a student designated as talented and gifted to receive additional and accelerated learning opportunities even in Advanced Placement classes.

Figure 6.3 COURSE OUTLINE—Advanced Placement Microeconomics

COURSE NUMBER   TBD
SCHOOL: Woodrow Wilson High School
INSTRUCTOR: Mark Marchese
CONTACT INFORMATION: mmarches@pps.k12.or.us
SUBJECT: Advanced Placement Microeconomics
DAYS OF THE WEEK OFFERED: Monday through Friday
HOURS OFFERED: Periods 1, 2, and 4
PREREQUISITE: Global Studies and United States History

COURSE DESCRIPTION: This college preparatory course undertakes an academically rigorous study of the principles of microeconomics to include the basic concepts of supply, demand, and product markets; factor markets, land, labor, and capital; and international trade.

LEARNING OBJECTIVES:

1. The course content will be the equivalent of at least eighteen weeks of university-level microeconomics.
2. All State of Oregon mandated instructional requirements will be met.
3. All Portland Public Schools mandated instructional requirements will be met.
4. All Oregon System of Higher Education admission requirements relative to economics will be met.
5. All College Board requirements in preparation for the Advanced Placement examination in microeconomics will be met.

TEXTBOOK: (Any state and school district approved economics text of your choice would be listed here.)

SCHEDULE OF TOPICS TO BE COVERED:
- Week 1 Economics, Microeconomics, and the Factors of Production
- Week 2 Scarcity, the Basic Economic Questions, Types of Economic Systems
- Week 3 The Economic Scheme, the Production Possibility Frontier, Trade-offs
- Week 4 Opportunity Cost, Efficiency, Scarcity, Adam Smith
- Week 5 The Law of Demand, the Law of Supply, Determinants of Demand, Determinants of Supply
- Week 6 The Circular Flow of the Economy, Public Goods, Externalities

Midterm Examination I

- Week 7 Price Ceilings and Price Floors, Market Failures, Demand vs. Quantity Demanded
- Week 8 Supply vs. Quantity Supplied; Shifts in Demand, Supply Equilibrium, Shortages and Surpluses
- Week 9 Price Elasticity of Demand, Price Elasticity of Supply, Utility, Consumer Surplus
- Week 10 The Paradox of Value, Production Functions, Total Product, Marginal Product, the Law of Diminishing Returns
- Week 11 Economies of Scale, Forms of Business Organization, Limited Liability
- Week 12 Total Cost, Total Revenue, Profit; Marginal Cost, Marginal Revenue, Average Cost, Average Revenue, and Profit Maximization

Midterm Examination II

- Week 13 Imperfect Competition and Profit Maximization, the Shutdown Rule, Industrial Concentration
- Week 14 Derived Factor Demand, Wages
- Week 15 Financial Investment vs. Real Investment
- Week 16 Sole Proprietorships, Partnerships, Corporations, Cooperatives
- Week 17 Monopoly vs. Monopsony
- Week 18 Final Examination

(continued)

Figure 6.3 *(continued)*

STUDENT ASSESSMENT: The following is a list of the assignments for the semester:

1. Weekly Written Article Reviews
2. Completion of Unit Study Guides
3. Midterm Examinations
4. Biographical Presentation
5. Composition Book of All Required Class Notes
6. Complete Portfolio of All Semester Work
7. Other as Student Needs Indicate

ADDITIONAL COSTS FOR MATERIALS: None.

SAFETY ISSUES AND REQUIREMENTS: Classroom safety is of paramount importance and will be always observed.

STUDENT ACCOMMODATIONS AND SUPPORT AVAILABLE:

1. As determined by 504 and/or IEP documents.
2. Daily tutoring Monday through Friday from 7:20 a.m. until 8:10 a.m. and on block schedule days from 1:58 p.m. until 2:40 p.m.

OPPORTUNITIES FOR FURTHER CHALLENGE:
Smith, Adam, *An Inquiry into the Nature and Causes of The Wealth of Nations*, Capstone Press, 2010, and written book review.
Keynes, John Maynard, *The General Theory of Employment, Interest, and Money*, Create Space Independent Publishing Platform, 2013, and written book review.
Hayek, Friedrich, *The Road to Serfdom*, University of Chicago Press, 2003, and written book review.
Friedman, Milton, *Free to Choose*, Mariner Books, 1990, and written book review.
Galbraith, John Kenneth, *The Affluent Society*, Penguin Press, 1999, and written book review.

FINAL THOUGHTS CONCERNING THE PLANNING OF INSTRUCTION FOR A NEW ACADEMIC YEAR

As a final thought, teachers are required to think, plan, and do when it comes to creating engaging lessons. Once the school year begins, most of your time is spent on direct student contact time. This leaves precious little time for planning and even less time for creative thinking. This points to the reality that summers become a natural place for leisurely creative thinking without the immediate daily demands of the school year upon you. Teachers should consider the benefits of using some time during summer vacations as instructional research and development time. One way to consider whether seasonal preplanning is right for you is by asking the question, "Would I rather work on preparing instruction's big ideas during a relaxed summer afternoon with an iced tea in my hand, or would I rather do it late on sleep-deprived and over-caffeinated weeknights and weekends during the school year?" Hopefully, the choice is clear.

QUESTIONS AND PRACTICES FOR CRITICAL THOUGHT

1. Explain why obtaining the school district's and school building's calendars for the current academic year are the first steps in the planning of instruction. Predict how classroom instruction could be impacted in the absence of these important documents.
2. A yearlong lesson plan is simply a list of subject matter topics to be taught within the time constraints of an academic year. Explain why this document is so important to teachers, students, parents, and administrators respectively.
3. We've discussed why the topics listed in a yearlong lesson plan may not merit equal amounts of instruction time. Cite examples of why this may be true for (a) mathematics (b) science (c) social studies, and (d) language arts classes.
4. Cite several reasons why it is advisable to have contingency lesson plans available for all levels of lesson planning. Further, cite several causes why over the course of an academic year it may

become necessary to truncate, or contract the length of, a yearlong lesson plan.
5. List and explain the component parts that constitute a quality course outline. Explain why this document is so important to teachers, students, parents, and administrators respectively.
6. It has been said that a course outline, especially when it relates to the class grading policy and student conduct, becomes a contract between teacher and students. Formulate an argument in favor of this position. Then, formulate an argument against this position.

DEVELOPMENTAL ACTIVITY NUMBER 6

1. Craft a yearlong lesson plan for a course that you teach or hope to teach.
2. Craft a course outline for a course that you teach or hope to teach.

Chapter 7

Planning Weekly Instruction

A goal without a plan is just a wish.

—Larry Elder

WHAT PREPARATION IS NEEDED TO CRAFT QUALITY WEEKLY LESSON PLANS?

Now that you've established a solid plan for a full academic year or semester of instruction that aligns perfectly with the prescribed curriculum, it is time to tighten your focus into a weekly lesson plan model of instruction and ultimately into a daily lesson plan model of instruction. It bears repeating that from your perspective as a classroom teacher, the prescribed curriculum is a given. Further, it will not be enough for any teacher to think that at this point they can arrive in a classroom, curriculum in hand, and by virtue of her or his charismatic personality impart the wisdom of the ages to a universally respectful audience that possesses an insatiable appetite for abstract knowledge. To the contrary, this is the point at which gaining command of what matters most in the teaching-learning process begins, mastering the art and science of pedagogy, which is most simply defined as the study of teaching methods.

There is an abundance of books and teacher training programs that address teaching methods and related topics. I recommend that every teacher in a PK–12 environment review the existing literature to independently identify sources that can inform weekly and daily instructional approaches that will be compatible with the nature of the assigned subject matter, individual teaching style, the developmental stage of the students, and most important, students' varied learning styles. At a minimum, your professional hardcopy tool kit should include your favorite book(s) on the following topics:

1. Learning theory (biological/psychological foundations of learning)
2. Lesson designs (nonsubject specific)
3. Models of teaching (subject specific)
4. Student management techniques

To add some clarification, for our purposes lesson design and models of teaching cannot be equated. A lesson design is the plan for the entire class session, while the model of teaching is a specific activity to teach and reinforce a specific concept, such as a titration lab within a chemistry class, a historiography project within a history class, or a team debate activity within an English class. And I want to make a special note regarding student management, more commonly referred to as keeping an orderly learning environment: the "secret" to controlling a classroom lies overwhelmingly in the quality of the lesson design. Let us take a closer look at how this might appear in action.

HOW IS A QUALITY WEEKLY LESSON PLAN TEMPLATE DEVELOPED?

After obtaining a blank teacher's lesson plan book, sketch out a minimally detailed plan, including date and topic for each day of the coming week. This should easily be established by the end of the day each Thursday. Refer to table 7.1.

Table 7.1   Teacher's Lesson Plan Book

September 12	September 13	September 14	September 15	September 16
Text Section 1.3 Review addition of whole numbers	Text Section 1.4 Review subtraction of whole numbers	Text Section 1.5 Review multiplication of whole numbers	Text Section 1.6 Review division of whole numbers Test preview	Test on whole numbers Begin chapter 2.1: Addition of mixed numbers

WHAT IS THE BEST USE OF A BLANK TEACHER'S LESSON PLAN BOOK?

It is helpful to examine an example of a real-world weekly lesson plan. Some teachers may refer to such a document as a "weekly syllabus," whereas some teachers may refer only to a course outline as a "syllabus." The word choice should be based on what all teachers at the same grade level agree on to preclude any unnecessary confusion on the students' part. I highly advise that you take the necessary time after school on Fridays to craft the next weekly lesson plan. That moment in time after school on Friday will allow you to know exactly where class progress left off for the week and where it is to begin the next Monday. Once written and finalized, the next step would be to make a paper copy for each student to be distributed on Monday at the beginning of class during the "preliminaries" phase. Additionally, posting the upcoming week's lesson plan on the class page on the school website helps to disseminate the information to a broader audience.

Following these steps in the lesson planning phase will ensure that advanced notice was given to students and parents alike, due process had been served, and no one could rely on the old and overused excuse of "But, you never told us about that assignment or when it was due!" Feel free to craft a personal model or recreate the model from figure 7.1 for your purposes. This figure displays an example of a weekly lesson plan for a grade seven social studies class. Notice the four components of the agenda element. Do bear in mind the value of an "assignment log" in addition to a weekly lesson plan. Keep this log in a common area where it is freely accessible to all students. The weekly lesson plan informs students and parents what is planned, and the assignment log records what was accomplished during a given class session by date. This documentation comes in very handy when students return from absences and ask, "What did I miss while I was gone?" The teacher can refer the students to the assignment log and eventually students will become conditioned to refer to the log first upon rejoining the class after any absence.

Figure 7.1 Weekly Lesson Plan for a Seventh Grade Social Studies Class

WEEK OF OCTOBER 23–27, 2017

- Lunch Bin Duty—Rachael and Gordon
- Playground Equipment Monitors—Cleo and Marc

MAJOR DUE DATES:

- Tuesday, October 24 (Date Firm) – Gandhi Biographical Presentation
- Thursday, October 26 (Target Date) – Completion of Unit I Geo Pack
- Friday, October 27 (Date Firm) – Current Event Due
- Monday, October 30 (Date Firm) – Chapter 4 Test
- Tuesday, November 21 (Date Firm) – Trimester 1 Book Reviews Due
- Tuesday, November 28 (Date Firm) – Makeup Work Cutoff Day
- Wednesday, November 29 (Date Firm) – Portfolios Due
- Thursday, November 30 (Date Firm) – Composition Books Due
- Friday, December 1 (Date Firm) – Last Day of Trimester 1

MONDAY, 10-23-17

1. Objective: To learn about understanding culture. (4.1)
2. Agenda:
   a. Preliminaries: Points of Information and Paper Return/Work Sample Files
   b. Direct Instruction: Chapter 4 Section 1
   c. Activity: Continue Unit 1 Geo Pack and Continue Group World Cartography Lab
   d. Homework: Current Event Prep, Book Review Reading, Biographical Presentation Prep

TUESDAY, 10-24-17

1. Objective: To learn about culture and society. (4.2)
2. Agenda:
   a. Preliminaries: Points of Information and Biographical Presentation
   b. Direct Instruction: Chapter 4 Section 2
   c. Activity: Continue Unit 1 Geo Pack and Continue Group World Cartography Lab
   d. Homework: Current Event Prep, Book Review Reading, Biographical Presentation Prep

WEDNESDAY, 10-25-17

1. Objective: To learn about cultural change. (4.3)
2. Agenda:
   a. Preliminaries: Points of Information
   b. Direct Instruction: Chapter 4 Section 3
   c. Activity: Continue Unit 1 Geo Pack and Continue Group World Cartography Lab
   d. Homework: Current Event Prep, Book Review Reading, Biographical Presentations

THURSDAY, 10-26-17

1. Objective: To review our knowledge of culture. (Chapter 4)
2. Agenda:
   a. Preliminaries: Points of Information, Geo Challenge, and DVD: TBD
   b. Direct Instruction: Chapter 4 Test Preview
   c. Activity: Continue Unit 1 Geo Pack and Continue Group World Cartography Lab
   d. Homework: Current Event Prep, Book Review Reading, Biographical Presentation Prep

(continued)

Figure 7.1 *(continued)*

> FRIDAY, 10-27-17
>
> 1. Objective: To learn more about international affairs and cultural geography.
> 2. Agenda:
>   a. Preliminaries: Points of Information and Current Events
>   b. Direct Instruction: National Geographic DVD
>   c. Activity: Continue Unit 1 Geo Pack and Continue Group World Cartography Lab
>   d. Homework: Current Event Prep, Book Review Reading, Biographical Presentation Prep

FINAL THOUGHTS ON PLANNING WEEKLY INSTRUCTION

Many times, American citizens will hear the phrase "due process." Generally, this phrase is used in a legal context. For example, procedural due process requires that a person be treated fairly by the government when being deprived of their life, liberty, or property. Substantive due process requires that laws be fair in the first place and that these laws justify a legitimate governmental purpose. I would like to introduce an additional and informal application of the concept of due process as "classroom due process." This concept in everyday real-world classroom practice could be tested by this simple question: When the child in question is faced with a reduction in grade or a zero grade, have they been treated fairly? At the core of this fairness test, in nearly 100 percent of cases, lies another question: Did the student receive advanced notice of the due date? By creating and disseminating a weekly lesson plan, both electronically and in paper form, that includes a complete listing of upcoming due dates, a teacher will find that due process has been served and consequently will reduce or eliminate any student or parent challenges on the grounds of absence of advanced notice.

QUESTIONS AND PRACTICES FOR CRITICAL THOUGHT

1. Define learning styles.
2. Conduct a brief internet search, then list and describe as many different types of learning styles as you can.
3. Explain why it is necessary for teachers to be familiar with the varied learning styles that students may possess. List and explain some of the varied challenges that teachers may face when crafting weekly lesson plans vis-à-vis the varied learning styles of their students.
4. How would you describe your own learning style as a student? In your opinion, was the instruction that you received compatible with your personal learning style?
5. Why would a teacher see value in keeping a personal library of resources related to teaching strategies? What four topics form the core and the minimum number of hardcopy resources forming a teacher's tool kit? Are there additional topical resources that you would consider adding to your personal teaching tool kit? If so, please provide a listing of these resources.
6. Explain the distinction between a lesson design and a model of teaching. Cite at least one example of each. Further, explain why it is important to incorporate both a lesson design and a model of teaching in a given class session.
7. Hypothetically place yourself in a teaching job interview. The principal asks you to describe the teaching-learning environment wherein students are "engaged" in a lesson. How would you answer? Further, explain how you would keep students engaged in the lessons that you would teach.
8. Do you agree that a nexus exists between a quality lesson design and an orderly teaching-learning environment in a classroom? Explain your reasoning.
9. Explain the difference between a blank teacher's calendar book and a blank teacher's lesson planning book. List and explain the two differing types of information that would be contained in each. Given these two layers of planning, list and explain the benefits of the additional step of producing and distributing a weekly lesson plan for each subject taught.

10. Describe an assignment log, and explain the purpose for keeping one. Further, explain the relationship between a lesson plan and an assignment log.

DEVELOPMENTAL ACTIVITY NUMBER 7

1. Craft a weekly lesson plan for a course that you teach or hope to teach.

Chapter 8

Planning Daily Instruction

Setting a goal is not the main thing. It is deciding how you will go about achieving it and staying with that plan.

—Coach Tom Landry

WHAT IS A CALM DAILY LESSON PLAN AND HOW IS IT CREATED?

CALM is an acronym for class activities lesson matrix. This daily lesson plan model consists of four major components: preliminary activities, direct instruction activities, workshop activities, and homework activities. See table 8.1.

A word about each of these components:

I. Preliminary Activities—This daily class component is an open forum that provides opportunity for a teacher to convey essential information to students concerning the expectations surrounding general attendance, academics, and citizenship issues. Most important among these issues may well be providing clear information about what has been assigned and when it is due.

Table 8.1 The Four Components of a Class Activities Lesson Matrix (CALM)

Preliminary Activities	Direct Instruction Activities
Workshop Activities	Homework Activities

But equally important, it is a time for students to ask clarifying questions about whatever is on their minds. This class component may take a greater or lesser amount of class time depending mostly upon the nature of upcoming assignments. However, time invested in this component is worth the dividends when it comes to elucidating the course of direction that has been set for the class and precluding any potential misunderstandings.

II. Direct Instruction Activities—This is the main event of the class session and should occur under a teaching and learning environment that provides for the highest levels of concentration while meeting the various learning styles of all students in the classroom. To help provide for such an atmosphere, I recommend projecting a detailed scroll of the following six Ls (6Ls) on the classroom screen. It would be wise to require each student to copy down exactly what they see on the screen into a personal class notebook that you assess for grading purposes later.

- Learning Target: The goal, objective, or content standard/substandard to be taught and fully understood by the students.
- Learning Starter: Often known as a "bell ringer" activity to engage the minds and attention of all students. By asking the students a starter question that utilizes higher order thinking skills, regardless of their age, they became engaged in rapid fashion. For instance, any question that requires their opinion, informed or not, compels the students to think quickly and to share their thoughts. Additionally, when it is time to hear the students' voluntary responses, it can be helpful to write their responses, correct or otherwise, on the board. This helps provide validation, creates a safe atmosphere in which to contribute to class interactions, and a basis for discernment. During this direct instruction piece, students need only write down their own response rather than responses of the other students.
- Learning Essentials: This point is where the essential vocabulary and information is delivered from teacher to students. A wide variety of delivery systems may be used, such as lectures, text readings, articles, guest speakers, visual presentations, student presentations, and so forth.
- Learning Assessment: This can be as simple as a five to ten question quiz over the learning essentials just presented. I would

Planning Daily Instruction 65

advise against using this assessment for grading purposes, but use it instead for the purpose of providing immediate feedback in the form of a self-check to each student concerning their recent comprehension and retention.
- Learning Reinforcement Activity: This piece can be as simple as textbook questions, a teacher prepared question/answer activity, or any creative device to reinforce what was just learned. You could use a line of questioning that utilizes various levels of learning and comprehension.
- Learning Closure Activity: For this final piece of direct instruction, you could double back and refer to the original Learning Target. If the students think that the learning target was hit, they may give a thumbs up; if not, they may give a thumbs down for instance.

III. Workshop Activities—After the direct instruction component has established the essential base of required knowledge, the workshop activities should reinforce this knowledge by moving into the realm of higher order tasks and critical thinking skills. Activities that are structured around comprehension and application can work quite successfully. This component can be interactive, hands-on, collaborative, or can take any creative path you want it to take relative to the given prescribed subject matter. This is an excellent time to bring additional models of teaching into effective action for conceptual reinforcement.

IV. Homework Activities—This component naturally encompasses tasks that require repetition for mastery such as the study of mathematics demands. Beyond that, this component inherently offers a space for long-term assignment progress and completion in terms of research, writing, and preparing for future examinations. If you work in a school that requires a prescribed number of minutes of homework per day per subject, this component easily meets that requirement without the dreadful and onerous nature that excessive skills drills present to tired students at the end of a day.

Please refer to table 8.2 for a detailed illustration of a CALM lesson plan. Notice the typical activities for each of the four components of the CALM format. The following pages will walk you through three sample lessons using the CALM method.

Table 8.2 Detailed Illustrations of a CALM Lesson Plan

I. Preliminary Activities
   A. Advanced Organizer
      1. General points of information and daily reminders
      2. Upcoming due dates reviewed
      3. Question and answer session about assignments and due dates
      4. Paper return and test review, and work sample file organization
      5. Daily quiz over previous class session's subject matter
      6. Student presentations
      7. Permission slips
      8. Other

II. Direct Instruction Activities
   A. Learning Target
   B. Learning Starter
   C. Learning Essentials
   D. Learning Assessment
   E. Learning Reinforcement Activity
   F. Learning Closure Activity

III. Workshop Activities
   A. Hands-on Activities
   B. Group Projects
   C. Labs
   D. Discussion Groups
   E. Other

IV. Homework Activities
   A. Long-range Assignments
   B. Examination Preparation
   C. Research and Writing
   D. Drill for Mastery

CALM DAILY LESSON PLAN
EXAMPLE A: THE WATER CYCLE

A. Learning Target: To learn about the water cycle.

TEACHER: "Please take out your class notebooks and copy down what you see on the screen."

TEACHER: "Today we are going to learn about the water cycle."

B. Learning Starter:

TEACHER: "I would like to take a public opinion survey. Please just raise your hand as we take the survey. At the point when we have the numerical results everyone will then have a chance to speak."

TEACHER: "We would like to know how people would prioritize the use of our limited water supplies in the western states when it comes to farming versus fish habitat."

TEACHER: "With a show of hands, how many of you think it is more important to use our limited water supply to protect salmon runs in our rivers than to divert the water to farms for irrigation?" (Teacher counts hands.)

TEACHER: "Now with a show of hands only, how many of you think it is more important to use our limited water supply to irrigate our farm crops than to protect salmon river runs?" (Teacher counts hands and places the final tally on the white board.)

TEACHER: "Please raise your hand if you would like to share your opinion."

(The teacher then designates an order for each student to share their opinion.)

C. Learning Essentials:

TEACHER: "Very well, thank you for your thoughts concerning the water cycle. Your thoughts were very insightful. Now let us look at some facts concerning the water cycle."

TEACHER: "Please copy these facts down in your notebook."

FACTS ABOUT THE WATER CYCLE:

1. The water cycle is the cycle of processes by which water circulates between the earth's oceans, atmosphere, and land, involving precipitation as rain and snow, drainage in streams and rivers, and return to the atmosphere by evaporation and transpiration.
2. An atmosphere is the layers of gasses surrounding a planet or other celestial body. Earth's atmosphere is composed of about 78 percent nitrogen, 21 percent oxygen, and 1 percent other gasses.
3. Precipitation is rain, snow, sleet, or hail that falls to the ground.
4. Evaporation is the process by which liquids turn into gases.
5. Transpiration is a plant's loss of water, mainly through the stomata of leaves.
6. Text reading: pages 19–24

D. Learning Assessment:

TEACHER: "Please close your textbooks and number one through five in your notebooks."

(The teacher projects and reads each question aloud twice.)

1. State the term used to describe the processes by which water circulates between the earth's oceans, atmosphere, and land, involving precipitation as rain and snow, drainage in streams and rivers, and return to the atmosphere by evaporation and transpiration.
2. State the term used to describe the layers of gasses surrounding a planet or other celestial body. Earth's atmosphere is composed of about 78 percent nitrogen, 21 percent oxygen, and 1 percent other gasses.
3. State the term used to describe the rain, snow, sleet, or hail that falls to the ground.
4. State the term used to describe the process by which liquids turn into gases.
5. State the term used to describe a plant's loss of water, mainly through the stomata of leaves.

TEACHER: "Thank you. Pencils down. If you have the answers, please raise your hand."

(The teacher then reads each question aloud and calls on individuals to respond, then thanks them for participating.)

E. Learning Reinforcement Activity:

TEACHER: "Let us continue with our Learning Reinforcement Activity. Please write down each question and your response to each in your class workbook."

(The teacher projects the following on the class screen.)

Please respond to each question below in your class notebook:

1. Define the water cycle.
2. Explain how the water cycle works.

3. Explain why an understanding of the water cycle is important if you are
   a. an independent farmer
   b. a government fish and wildlife manager
   c. a biology researcher at a university
   d. an independent landscape contractor
4. List and explain at least three factors that might affect the behavior of the water cycle.
5. Draw a detailed and colorful diagram of the water cycle.

F. **Learning Closure Activity:**

TEACHER: "Our learning target for today was to learn about the water cycle. If you think that we hit our learning target, show us a thumbs up. If you think that we missed our learning target, show us a thumbs down. Thank you."

CALM DAILY LESSON PLAN
EXAMPLE B: THE EIGHT PARTS OF SPEECH

A. Learning Target: To learn about the eight parts of speech and to be able to give examples of each.

B. Learning Starter:

Based on your current knowledge, and without consulting any sources, list the eight parts of speech and give at least one example of each part of speech.

Part of Speech: Example:

1.   1.
2.   2.
3.   3.
4.   4.
5.   5.
6.   6.
7.   7.
8.   8.

C. Learning Essentials: The eight parts of speech and examples of each are as follows:

Part of Speech:	Function:	Example:
1. Noun	Person, place, or thing	June, Beijing, car
2. Verb	Action word	Cook, work, play
3. Adjective	Modifies a noun	Windy city
4. Adverb	Modifies a verb	Run fast
5. Preposition	Shows relationship between words	Book on the shelf
6. Pronoun	Replaces nouns	him, her, you, me
7. Conjunction	Joins words, phrases, or clauses	Ramon is musical and athletic.
8. Interjection	Shows strong feelings	Wow! What happened?

D. Learning Assessment: True or False?

1. In the sentence, "Monique is an Honor Roll student," the name *Monique* is a pronoun. True or False
2. In the sentence, "Randy ran all the way from Redding to Richmond," the word *ran* is a verb. True or False
3. In the sentence, "Julia pitches faster than Rosa," the word *faster* is an adjective. True or False
4. In the sentence, "The shiny car was speeding," the word *shiny* is an adverb. True or False
5. In the sentence, "The spare tire is in the trunk," the word *in* is a preposition. True or False
6. In the sentence, "You and I will be going later," the words *you* and *I* are pronouns. True or False
7. In the sentence, "I will wait politely until dinner is served," the word *until* is a conjunction. True or False
8. In the sentence, "Ouch! That hurt!" The word *ouch* is an interjection. True or False

E. Learning Reinforcement Activity:

Craft a single paragraph that includes at least one example for each of the eight parts of speech.
 Any volunteers for sharing their paragraph aloud?

F. Learning Closure Activity:

Thumbs up or thumbs down?

CALM DAILY LESSON PLAN
EXAMPLE C: CULTURES OF THE WORLD

A. Learning Target: To learn about how to understand other cultures. (4.1)

B. Learning Starter:

Based on your current knowledge, write a one sentence definition of the term *culture*.

C. Learning Essentials

1. Culture is an entire way of life that is shaped by people's environment; the way of life then also shapes people's environment, this includes their beliefs and practices.
2. Culture developed over time from simple technologies and institutions to more advanced technologies and institutions.
3. Cultural landscape is the part of a people's environment that they have shaped and the technology they used to shape it.
4. Civilization is an advanced culture with cities and a system of writing.
5. An institution is a custom or organization with social, educational, or religious purposes.
6. Text reading: pages 92–95

D. Learning Assessment:

1. State the term used to describe the way of life of a people, including their beliefs and practices.
2. State the term used to describe the parts of a people's environment that they have shaped and the technology they have used to shape it.
3. State the term used to describe an advanced culture with cities.
4. True or False: *culture* and *society* are synonymous.

E. Learning Reinforcement Activity:

An institution is a custom or organization with social, educational, or religious purposes. In groups of four as assigned by the teacher, create a small mural depicting at least three institutions from other cultures besides our own.

F. Learning Closure:

Journal writing.

FINAL THOUGHTS ON PLANNING DAILY INSTRUCTION

Creating a CALM written lesson plan for each class one teaches may seem time-consuming and repetitive on the surface. Rest assured that the benefits of doing so far outweigh the costs measured in terms of time and effort on the part of the teacher. It has been said many times by many people that there are no shortcuts to success. With enough practice, one will develop the ability to create direct instruction lessons in extemporaneous fashion, which may come in handy when called to cover a class for a colleague who is experiencing an emergency but has left no lesson plan.

DEVELOPMENTAL ACTIVITY NUMBER 8

Craft a daily lesson plan for a single class session using a class activities lesson matrix for a class that you currently teach or hope to teach. Please include specific elements during the sample Preliminary Activities, a specific model for use in the Direct Instruction Activities, a specific conceptual reinforcement model of teaching in the Workshop Activities, and specific samples of long-term assignments for use during the Homework Activities.

Chapter 9

Creating a Productive Classroom Learning Environment

Baseball is 90 percent mental; the other half is physical.

—Yogi Berra

WHY IS A TEACHER'S MINDSET IMPORTANT?

Frankly stated, keeping order in the classroom is job number one. If order is not established, all is lost. This may be accomplished through sheer force of personality. For example, a young preservice teacher told of a field experience at the middle school level with a cooperating teacher who was a retired US Navy commander aptly named Mr. Steele. Once retired from his distinguished service to our country, Mr. Steele decided that public school teaching would be his next avenue of contributing to the public good. He stood straight and tall in the classroom at about six foot five, possessed a totally bald pate along with long, thick gray eyebrows that were Butch waxed and curled into something resembling eagle wings. He owned a laser-beam stare and would spend entire class sessions patrolling the isles between student desks with a yardstick in one hand while expounding in detail the finer points of physical geography. He spoke in dynamics, which included a voice that would make the classroom windows rattle. This man could have made the building principal's chin quiver. Nary a word out of place, nor a single immature act, ever occurred in Mr. Steele's classroom. Also, needless to say, very few teachers are ever gifted by Mother Nature with such an intimidating persona as Mr. Steele. Hence, in the process of creating a productive classroom learning environment, it becomes essential for every teacher to possess something more universal: a lesson plan design that is superior in engaging students. Such a model, the class activities lesson matrix, or CALM design model, was introduced in chapter 8.

This model offers students something more enticing to devote their sometimes-limited attention to versus the shiny allure of disruptive activity. Consequently, expect such a lesson plan design to preclude off-task behaviors at a high rate. But more valuable than a unique persona or superior class plans is a teacher's mindset before ever teaching that first minute.

HOW IS A CORRECT TEACHER'S MINDSET CREATED?

First, all teachers must like kids. If a person decides to pursue a career in PK–12 teaching for whatever reason yet doesn't particularly care for children or being around them, then the game is over before it starts. A veteran principal during a teacher in-service day told his faculty that they must like kids and must cheerily greet them at the classroom door before every class session but especially on that first day of school. His rationale being that kids have a sixth sense when it comes to teachers, and as he put it, "Within the first ten seconds of meeting you they know if you like kids or not and the stage is set from there." If you think back as a child on your own K–12 student experience, you would probably admit to possessing this same sixth sense that is quick to render summary judgments labeling teachers as "nice" or "mean." This is a very good example of how the mind of a child works. To a young person, "mean" usually can be reduced to the subjective equivalent of not liking children, and if a teacher does not like kids it becomes rapidly and unmistakably apparent. On the other hand, delighting in young people and interacting with them doesn't take much effort or special training. For instance, while teaching in a K–8 school, a teacher had his planning period before the middle school lunch but during the primary grades lunch. Each day on his way to check his mailbox in the office, he would make it a habit to swing through the cafeteria for a quick chat with the littles. After telling the middle school teacher everything they did that morning, everything they were eating for lunch, what their cat did yesterday, and why their mom is mad, he once attempted to get a word in edgewise. He jokingly told the kids at the table that he had a night job and that he was Batman from midnight until six in the morning and fought crime in his fifty-five-year-old and older neighborhood. This was met with giggles from mouths full of sandwiches. But one second grade girl said, "I don't believe that for a minute!" The middle school teacher asked her, "Oh, and why not?" She responded, "Because your eyes already look too tired to stay up all night!" He laughed and was in a joyous mood for the rest of the afternoon. The innocence, candor, and humor kids can bring to the moment is priceless. Once while waiting too long for an assembly to begin, a colleague of mine noticed two second grade girls getting restless with the delay. To distract them from potential mischief the teacher asked the two their ages. One student proudly said, "I'm eight!" The other sheepishly responded, "Seven." The teacher then randomly asked them if they could guess her age. The first student sharply replied, "twenty-eight!" The second student said, "forty-nine!" The veteran primary teacher informed the young ladies, "I'm sixty-three years old." Through wide grins and with great joviality, the two students exclaimed in unison "Eeewwww!" Again, the teacher's laughter could not be contained, and neither could the laughter of the two students thinking themselves such exceptional comedians. These interactions may not have brought the same joy to some teachers as they brought to these two teachers, but it is obvious they liked and enjoyed the unpredictable and lighthearted interactions that kids provide.

WHY DOES THE CORRECT TEACHER MINDSET NECESSITATE HAVING ENTHUSIASM FOR YOUR WORK?

An example of having enthusiasm for one's work could be exemplified in one teacher's periodic moments of classroom exuberance to his students, "Most people get up in the morning and say, 'I have to go to work today . . . ' When I get up in the morning I say, 'I GET to go to work today!" Words of this type send a message to kids. This teacher claimed to have the great fortune of teaching Advanced Placement Microeconomics and Macroeconomics. This was a unique claim against the backdrop of the Scottish essayist and historian Thomas Carlyle once terming the study of economics the "dismal science" due to economist Thomas Malthus's grim prediction that the world population would ultimately outgrow world food supply. Etiology notwithstanding, most economics students associated the phrase "dismal science" with one or two semesters of convoluted and wearisome required course content. But to him the study of economics served as a portal to a deeper and applied understanding of the workings of all the other social sciences, behavioral sciences, business models, money, and mathematics. One student of his once independently observed, "Economics causes calculus to make sense and calculus causes the study of economics to make sense." While most high school social studies teachers dread the thought of being assigned to teach even one section of economics, for him it was fascinating. He claimed that the more knowledge of economics he acquired, the more he desired. Before he knew it, he was teaching before and after school economics study sessions and getting the students into teams and traveling for interscholastic economics competitions. His classes became a factory for future economics majors. The students were having a blast and he was having a blast! Obviously, he was the right person in the right place. During one of his annual evaluations the administrator noted that his students are enthusiastic about the study of economics because he is enthusiastic about economics. It was also vividly apparent in every classroom up and down the halls of this high school that the teachers liked their students and were on fire for their subject matter. This combination makes for a wonderful teaching and learning atmosphere. There is no doubt that the students in this school were happier to go to school each day knowing that their teachers were happy to see and teach them with great enthusiasm.

WHY DOES THE CORRECT TEACHER MINDSET NECESSITATE REALISTIC THINKING?

To begin, teachers must be realistic in their expectations of themselves. A classroom teacher is just that, a teacher, meaning they are a licensed expert in their subject matter, child development, the delivery of age-appropriate instruction, and the supervision of all students in their charge. They play a large role in the lives of their students. On the other hand, a teacher is not a friend, professional social worker, police officer, attorney, family mediator, child psychologist, psychiatrist, nor a physician. Professional all-purpose problem solvers do not exist, nor care as much as teachers do; to attempt to become one even momentarily is professional overreach. A professional division of labor exists for good reasons. When a teacher senses that any given student is troubled by problems that extend beyond their scope of expertise, range of authority, or printed responsibilities, they should go directly to the school counselor or any building administrator and express their concern.

Next, this point is stated with special emphasis, teachers are mandatory reporters. That is, all teachers must report even *suspected* child abuse or child neglect to their building principal and local police or state child welfare services. Failure to do so makes a teacher liable to sanctions to include the possibility of revocation of their state teaching license. Laws regarding this vary by state so you should check your state statutes regarding this and take your responsibilities in this realm very seriously. But I can offer two real-world examples that are at variance. First example, as the bell rang ending morning "reg-room," a teary-eyed student came up to the teacher, lifted their shirt, and exposed belt welts on the rib area that resulted from an "alleged" assault by a sibling. Suspected child abuse? No question. The student was consoled, given time to regain composure, and sent on to period 1 class. The teacher then went directly to the principal's office to relay the story and together they placed a call into Children and Family Services and then informed the school counselor. The teacher's outrage with this obvious abuse notwithstanding, the teacher's professional responsibilities had been fulfilled at this point and it was now time to continue remaining professional by henceforth keeping the event confidential. Second example, while delivering direct instruction a teacher noticed a student taking notes who had multiple bruise marks on the inside and outside of the upper arms, much like you would expect to see after one had been grabbed by the arms and squeezed by an angry person. After class the teacher discreetly asked the student about the bruises. The student cheerily told the teacher that they were the result of last Saturday's judo tournament in which they had won divisional first place. Quickly and proudly the student produced a picture showing the said student on the victory stand with a medal in place. Suspected child abuse? Nope. Congratulations and have a nice day!

Additionally, a teacher must be realistic in the expectations that they place on students. In a perfect world, every student desk and chair would be the workstation of a fully prepared, attentive, focused, respectful, and perfectly mature young person just waiting to always learn and please the teacher. However, a perfect world is not where we live. You should always remind yourself that kids are going to do the things that kids do, so be prepared to experience the behavioral characteristics of the age group you teach. This is where a full understanding of the range of human development is very helpful. If you stop to think about it, a newborn is completely dependent on adults; they are self-centered, impatient, and impulsive. Over the years as an infant grows and develops into adulthood, these behavioral characteristics gradually diminish and new ones emerge. All PK–12 students are on this road of development, and they have not reached full adulthood yet. Teachers need to be patient, set behavioral boundaries, offer guidance, and remember that they are the adults in the room. Additionally, it is essential to remember that every student arrives at school affected, for better or worse, by variables in their personal lives that are too broad and deep to be delineated, let alone discussed here. Every student also arrives at school affected, for better or worse, by variables in how they learn in a classroom setting. This latter fact is much easier to work with because it is not as varied or as distant as the myriad of exogenous life issues that may affect a student's academic performance. Always keep in mind that each student will learn differently. From informal observation it becomes rapidly apparent that most students are visual learners. Strong auditory learners are rare and often present themselves as uninterested in the lesson, declining to take notes, reading a book during direct instruction, and appearing disengaged while absorbing each word and concept spoken and presented by the teacher. Consequently, it becomes pedagogically paramount to touch on all modalities of learning when delivering direct instruction. If each student is involved in a manner of direct instruction that requires, or at least offers, hearing and concurrently seeing the material, and writing and parroting back the material presented, great progress is made toward satisfying individual student learning styles in collective and efficient fashion. For students who are given the opportunity to see *and* hear *and* write *and* speak during the direct instruction process, not supplanting individual education plans (IEPs) and/or differentiated instruction but working in concert with them, great learning strides can and will occur. A word of caution is in order at this juncture. Teachers have a strong tendency to teach either visually or auditorily depending on how well they learned as a student. Always remember to cover all learning styles.

Further, be prepared for instructional disruptions. They will happen, don't let them frustrate you. There will be random fire drills, assemblies, late openings, early dismissals, weather closures, illness outbreaks, individual student requests to make a restroom trip, and of course at the very moment of reaching a given lesson's crescendo phase and the unit's climactic point, the intercom comes on and interrupts your intellectual grandiloquence with the secretary's voice asking, "Would you send 'Little Johnny' to the office, his mother is here to pick him up early"—the ultimate momentum breaker!

Finally, keep the mindset of "I will find a way to make every situation end well" and never stop thinking of ways to make that happen. A former high school football coach shared that a certain number of problems will occur for both the home team and the opponent's team during any game. Both would experience fumbles, interceptions, injuries, blown coverages, missed blocks and tackles, and penalties. Kids are humans not machines. But he maintained that the team that would ultimately win was the team that was best at overcoming the difficulties presented. The same applies to life in general and to the classroom. If a student falls behind for whatever reason, find a way for him or her to catch up. If ten days of instruction are lost for whatever reason during a semester, find a way to get the material covered anyway. If new textbooks are on backorder and will not arrive until mid-October, find alternative readings to use. If most of a class does not meet with success on an examination, remediate, reteach, and reexamine. If the last class of the day consists of a disproportionate number of particularly obstreperous youngsters, find a way to channel their energies into productive outcomes. In all instances, you should be committed to finding ways to make every situation end well and soon you will find that your experiences have left you with the gift of multiple strategies that can be applied in overcoming new and familiar problems as they occur.

WHAT ARE SOME DOS AND DON'TS FOR THE CLASSROOM TEACHER IN ACTION?

Let's face it. As classroom teachers we are always outnumbered by something around thirty to one. We should indeed like this fact. Twenty to forty-two students each full of energy, intelligence, and wily as a fox—often with a thirty to ninety minute personal agenda of their own that may, or may not, be harmonic with the one the teacher has set for the class time. The teacher's job is always to get out in front of all possible situations before they even occur and "outfox the foxes" by keeping them focused and engaged in productive academic activity from bell to bell—yes, even after fire drills and/or pep assemblies. President Theodore Roosevelt is credited with the quote, "A small change can make a big difference." So let's look at some small changes that you can put in a your classroom toolbox that *do* make a big difference.

Do:

- Create security for your students. There are many ways in which this can be accomplished. Some ways include, but are not limited to, establishing a calm, confident, and professional command presence; having self-control; being organized; being consistent; being fair and equitable in all matters; being a subject matter expert; being well prepared; practicing what you preach; keeping a classroom that is physically orderly, organized, clean, and tidy; establishing regular classroom routines and responsibilities especially in the primary, intermediate, and middle grades; and making expectations and directions clear both in writing and auditorily.
- Meet every student at the door of your classroom as they arrive. This provides for a pleasant tone before class begins as well as enables you to monitor events happening in the hallway and in the classroom. The students will know that you are constantly in supervision mode and therefore they will be less likely to practice

the fine art of mischief making. Additionally, if possible, try to individually acknowledge each student in some way at some point each day. Offer praise for a job well done, have informal chats about some professional sports team that you both follow, assist a student academically, but somehow offer some personal acknowledgment daily. No child wants to feel invisible; children crave the notice and approval of their teachers. If a child does feel invisible, their self-worth is affected and may seek the desired acknowledgment through negative means.

- Begin class proceedings immediately when the tardy bell rings. Physical and auditory signals that teachers send can be helpful in indicating to students that it is time to be on task. If you are on task, students are more likely to be on task. As a practical example given by one teacher, when the tardy bell would ring, she would close the classroom door and state, "We begin!" She would then walk to front and center and engage the students until the next bell would ring. As another example, while teaching advanced high school students in a lecture intensive course during a 105-minute block, one teacher would provide planned periodic seven-minute in-class breaks. The lights were off for the lecture since visuals were projected and the lights were on for the in-class break; when the lights were once again turned off it meant back to work. This proved quite effective in providing a successful transition.
- Take accurate attendance. This is extremely important. A teacher's attendance records could even be subpoenaed by a court if needed, so it is indeed a significant professional responsibility. You will find it helpful to have an assigned student seating chart and a silent student writing activity, such as a starter question or quiz, early during class proceedings. Not only will it allow for quick and accurate attendance recording, but it will also be an excellent technique to focus the students' attention on the learning process.
- Teach bell to bell. This means you will need to plan not only for direct instruction and curriculum-related activities, but for meaningful, purposeful, and structured nonacademic activities as well. These activities may include brain breaks to allow students to reset as previously mentioned. Examples include primary grades having regularly scheduled after lunch quiet time/nap time as well as middle grades getting a "take five" with heads down on their desks

and lights off; these are surprisingly welcomed by the students and effective in fostering a calmer class period. But in any case, you should never allow unplanned time during a class session.
- Make transitions from task to task seamless whenever practical. In essence, create overlapping activities. For example, "When you have completed the reading, silently take out your geography packet and continue on with your progress."
- Teach on your feet whenever practical. Proximity to the students is one of the most effective means of precluding and preventing off-task behavior by students. Circulating the classroom constantly and being equally involved in the lesson as a participant with the kids is important. As a practical example, you will find it quite helpful to use a rolling cart as an auxiliary desk. Equipped with a laptop computer, Bluetooth mouse, and connection to a projection system, you will have a "mobile teaching and command center" that could move anywhere in the room as needed. This will provide an effective tool during direct instruction, student presentations, student grade conferences, and lab activities.
- Give advanced notice on everything. One of the most important components of due process is advanced notice. Any teacher knows that one of the most common ploys students use in order to avoid responsibility for an assignment is the good old, "But you didn't tell us about that assignment!" and its ignoble derivative of "But you didn't tell us when that was due!" The saddest part of this ruse is that far too often one parent will accept their child's subterfuge as truth or at least accept it as a way of buying extra time for an assignment to be completed to preclude a low grade. To prevent this annoying scenario from unfolding, or stopping it cold when it does occur, you should personally distribute into the hand of each student during Monday morning class preliminaries a hardcopy of the current week's lesson plan. This document should be replete with a listing of all assignments and their due dates. Don't forget to hold copies with the names of any absent students for distribution whenever the absentees should return. It is strongly recommended that you post the same information on the classroom web page for the parents to see. In introductory teacher education courses, students are often told by their professor, "The most important thing I could ever tell you is to tell the students what it is you are

going to tell them, then tell them, then tell them what you have told them." Once teachers begin their professional career, this advice will prove to be quite sage indeed. When disseminating exceptionally important information, one of my particularly animated colleagues would place his index fingers on his temples and say to the students, "Put your fingers to your brain and repeat after me. Chapter 7 test is this coming Friday!" and the student chorus would respond, "Chapter 7 test is this coming Friday!" After such exhaustive advance notice, it became unlikely that any student would descend to the level of "But you didn't tell us the test was Friday!" But if it did happen, it would be completely unnecessary for the teacher to respond because the heedless student's peers would enthusiastically offer thoughtful encouragement concerning paying better attention in class in the future.

- Teach vocabulary first. When beginning a new unit of instruction, or even a new lesson, it is very important to teach any new vocabulary before delving into the new content. This seems obvious. High level, specialized, or even familiar terms that may carry unique academic contexts might seem ordinary and second nature to a teacher, especially in the upper grades, but perhaps are unheard of to the students. It is not out of the question that a student who is not familiar with any given vocabulary word would avoid asking for clarification out of fear of drawing attention to themselves, lack the motivation to consult the glossary, or assume the vocabulary word pairs with an incorrect definition. Without a complete understanding of a subject matter's vocabulary, forward learning is impeded and may lead to frustration in the learner, which may lead to a suboptimal learning outcome.
- Return papers during seatwork. Paper return should not occur in a learning vacuum because it is not an instructional activity and therefore would fail under any circumstance to fully engage the students with productive activity. An instructional void would be created, which is a lost teaching-learning opportunity; instead, it becomes an opportunity for off-task student behavior because there simply is no task. If possible, paper returns should occur while students are otherwise occupied by engaging activities like silent reading.

- Display student work in the classroom. This not only reinforces positive student self-images, but it also provides an incentive for students to produce their very best work. Additionally, your classroom will present as an active and positive environment in which a high degree of learning takes place.
- Change up classroom learning activities often. Conventional wisdom tells us that the expected attention span of children is approximately one minute focus for each year of their age. Therefore, with a sixth grade class, you should have four or more different learning activities for a standard fifty-minute class.

Henry Ford is credited with the quote, "The only real mistakes we make in life are the ones from which we learn nothing." So let's look at some of the little mistakes teachers commonly make, and may not even be aware of, and be watchful for them.

Don't:

- End a sentence with "OK?" while directing a class. For example, "Students please take out your notebooks, OK?" To tack on the interjection OK? is not only superfluous, but it also sends the false message to the students that you are somehow seeking their permission for something to happen or at least hoping for their generous compliance with the directive.
- Say, "Shhhhh!" when attempting to bring the class to order. Be assured that if you tell the class to "Shhhhh" once, you will have to tell the class to "Shhhhh" multiple times during a given class period, each time to no effect. Find alternatives that are preferably nonverbal so as not to diminish your authoritative presence if not immediately responded to. Lower grade teachers have great success with the technique of rhythmically clapping five times. Consider this an opportunity to perhaps introduce American Sign Language or another system of hand signage.
- Assign reading assignments as homework, especially on a regular basis. The rationale here is that students will not read what is assigned as homework. Even if the assigned reading is to be followed by a quiz at the start of the next class (which by the way is an excellent technique to bring a class to initial order), you will find that compliance will remain minimal or even nonexistent. The

only way to be certain that all students have completed assigned readings is to read aloud in class and discuss the material at intervals while progressing through the reading. Not only will you know that at least each student present completed the necessary readings, you will also find students of all ages are receptive to this practice and that a superior dialogue between student and student, as well as between students and teacher, will result from such an instructional activity.
- Allow students to hand in papers directly to the your desk. Students may place assignments anywhere on your desk, especially if the desk is messy. Additionally, the old trick of not turning an assignment in at all and then saying that they turned it into the teacher's desk may be at play. This well-used ploy, hatched in the mind of a child whose strategic thinking is more advanced than their ethical development, is a stratagem that has skillfully transferred the onus of responsibility for the assignment from themselves to the teacher. In other words, they no longer must prove that they turned the assignment in, but rather it is now up to the teacher to prove that they didn't. A preferred practice is to circulate the classroom, staple, and collect work from students individually. If a student does not have an assignment to turn in at the designated time, the teacher-student discussion would occur immediately, and you can record the event in writing on the spot. An email home to the parents would follow. However, it is an allowable practice to maintain a turn-in basket on your desk for makeup work only. This may sound controlling, but consider designating you as the only person to use the stapler. If students are allowed the privilege of using the stapler, when one person gets out of their seat to use the device, one by one, the rest of the class is soon out of their seat to use the stapler too. Additionally, students will commonly use multiple staples when one will suffice, use their fist in hammer-like fashion to operate the stapler causing damage, as well as to staple things not intended to be stapled. When not in use, the stapler should remain in a drawer in your desk.
- Send students to the office for behavioral issues unless a safety issue is involved. Think proactively and be prepared to preclude, or at least remedy, individual student's episodes of substandard citizenship that may occur from time to time. There are many

reasons for this piece of advice, but suffice it to say that if you do send a student to the office, at the least, you have inadvertently abdicated your authority over the student and sent him or her the clear message that you are now officially incapable of securing said student's cooperation in the classroom. However, it is nevertheless essential that if a given student begins to manifest disruptive classroom behavior, the parents and administrators become informed at the soonest possible moment. However, it is not only acceptable, but desirable, to secure parental and administrative support in your lead efforts to assist the student in achieving improved deportment. A word of caution is in order at this point, when informing parents and/or administrators of arising problems, it is of paramount importance for you to project perfect calmness, objectivity, and professionalism while describing the problematic behaviors. As a teacher, projecting agitation will no doubt elicit a similar response from one or more of the involved adults. In efforts to extinguish occasional substandard student behavior, success can be found in using the following techniques: (1) While in the process of instructing the class and patrolling the isles, stop aside the mild disruptor's desk and simply tap an index finger three times on their desk without any other student's being aware, nor allowing for any break in your instructional rhetoric. (2) Place the disruptor in a separate area, yet clearly in your line of sight for supervision purposes and inform them at any point they feel they are ready to rejoin the class without drawing negative attention to themselves they are welcome to return. (3) Summon certain students to your desk to silently watch you compose an email to the student's parents describing in detail their child's behaviors that are preventing the other students from learning. Then ask the offender if it is necessary for you to push the send button. Students will invariably and immediately tell you it is not. At which point inform the student that you will keep the email in your drafts for potential future use as needed. (4) In the more problematic cases, without advance notice to the student, you may decide to summon the parent(s) for a same-day appointment after school with their student to be present. At the meeting you can calmly delineate in detail a listing of the behaviors demonstrated by the student that are clearly unacceptable for a classroom setting. This technique is highly successful in the remediation of problem behaviors and invariably proves to be an emotional experience for both parent and student. (5) As a final example, and only after securing permission from the principal in advance, inform the disruptive student and her or his parents that if immediate improvement is not realized then the student will not be allowed back in class without a parent being present in the classroom with the student the remainder of the semester. Please note that no public confrontation occurred in any of these examples. In-class showdowns between teacher and student are rarely productive. At best, both participants will experience a lower approval rating in the eyes of the other students present. At worst, the student involved may become a bit of a folk hero to his peers, a Robin Hood–type figure.

- Be alone with a student in a classroom with a closed door. When providing additional help to a student before or after school or during lunchtime, you should only seek to do so in a common area like the cafeteria or a foyer. If an otherwise empty classroom must be used, at the very least keep the classroom door wide open and inform a colleague of the meeting in advance.

FINAL THOUGHTS REGARDING THE CREATION OF A PRODUCTIVE CLASSROOM LEARNING ENVIRONMENT

All teachers were once children themselves, and as such would no doubt often consult their own parents for situational advice. It is the nature of parents to be quite generous in dispensing sage wisdom when asked or perhaps even when not asked. Much of this inherited wisdom still serves their adult children well even to this day. At other times parents may straightforwardly offer their child the incurious directive of, "Well, I guess you will just have to put on your 'thinking cap' and figure this one out for yourself." So it is with the classroom teaching process. You should feel free to consult not only the senior teachers you know, but any teacher for whom you have respect. Ask how they handle given situations and classroom routines, then pick and choose from what they have to offer. The more proactive strategies that you have at your disposal, the fewer reactive strategies you will need. Nevertheless, it is necessary to plan for both types of strategies because no matter how long your career spans, you will always encounter situations you haven't seen before. You should make every attempt to keep your repertoire of proactive strategies greater in number than your repertoire of reactive strategies. But any time a reactive strategy is used, analyze it, convert what you have learned into a new proactive strategy, and refine it for future use. Be assured that a student's mind never rests, so neither can yours. Keep the thinking cap close at hand.

QUESTIONS AND PRACTICES FOR CRITICAL THINKING

1. Place yourself in a hypothetical interview for a teaching position. The principal asks you, "Describe the ideal classroom teaching and learning environment. Further, how would you go about creating such an atmosphere?" How would you respond?
2. A teacher's mindset is important before even entering into a classroom setting. How would you describe a correct teacher mindset? Further, how would you go about getting into the correct "headspace" for leading a classroom full of students?
3. List and explain the benefits of teacher enthusiasm for children and for subject matter.
4. The correct teacher mindset necessitates realistic thinking and expectations. How do you interpret this statement? Give a hypothetical example of a teacher applying realistic thinking.
5. It is a fair assessment to say that educators are in general an idealistic group of people. It is also fair to say that realistic thinking grows as an educator becomes more experienced. In your opinion, where can the balance be found between this idealistic and realistic thinking?
6. What are your state's laws as applied to teachers reporting suspected child abuse? Give at least one hypothetical example of an incidence of suspected child abuse and describe what course of action you would take in that event. For practical purposes, how would you interpret the term *suspected* in the phrase "suspected child abuse?"

7. Professionals can identify many different types of student learning styles. However, in the common classroom setting when it comes to absorbing subject matter during direct instruction, teachers will generally see the characteristics of either auditory learning or visual learning predominantly manifested. Explain how you, in a classroom teaching capacity, could simultaneously meet the needs of students who possess one or the other of these styles.
8. From this chapter's listing of Dos and DON'TS, cite what you consider to be the first and foremost from each of these categories. Provide rationale for your choices.

DEVELOPMENTAL ACTIVITY NUMBER 9

Develop a Next Semester/Next Year file to keep in the top right-hand drawer of your teacher desk. Use this file as a repository of notes that you have written to yourself containing ideas about how you can make changes, or experiment with ideas that may make your classroom a better teaching and learning environment.

Chapter 10

Teacher–Parent Communications

Good communication is the bridge between confusion and clarity.

—Nat Turner

WHY IS COMMUNICATION BETWEEN TEACHERS AND PARENTS IMPORTANT?

The importance of good communication cannot be overstated. Good lines of clear, timely, and complete communication to all concerned within a K–12 institution serves to clarify a course of direction, unify people behind completion of goals and objectives, minimize potential misunderstandings and their accompanying conflicts, and send to all recipients the message that they are valued and respected as participants in the greater teaching and learning process.

Let us assume for the moment that all school internal communication is as it should be. Since the primary responsibility for internal communication rests with administration, that places discussion on that component outside of the scope of this writing. So let us focus solely on teacher–parent communication. It is fair to say, and simple to understand, that parents are most likely to express displeasure when presented with delayed information about their child having problematic attendance, behavior, and/or academic performance issues. This is especially true when the bad news is first delivered by the report card.

If you hope to keep parents as valuable team members, you must share clear, timely, and complete information concerning any problematic behaviors manifested by their child.

The available delivery methods of communication are many and efficient. Any time an attendance, behavioral, or academic issue arises, please make immediate contact with the parent(s) via regularly scheduled progress reports, emails, or the old-fashioned personal phone call. Since the semester or annual parent–teacher conference days are the greatest opportunity for in-depth communication, as we progress through this chapter we'll focus on the sequential mechanics of this event.

WHY SHOULD PARENT–TEACHER CONFERENCES BE EAGERLY ANTICIPATED?

Any teacher has reason to look forward to a parent–teacher conference with a great sense of optimism. This contact presents a valuable opportunity for several objectives to be accomplished: (1) parents can obtain a focused and clear assessment of their child's overall classroom performance, (2) parents can obtain a firsthand knowledge of their child's teacher as a professional as well as a human in this uninterrupted and focused environment, (3) teachers can possibly obtain a greater knowledge of any external factors, if a parent chooses to share them, that may be affecting a student's academic and/or social experiences, (4) teachers can take this as an opportunity to build trust with parents by showcasing her or his professionalism. The following sections highlight some specific points of preparation that will help to ensure a successful experience for both parent and teacher.

HOW CAN A CORE SUBJECT MATTER TEACHER BE PROPERLY PREPARED FOR PARENT–TEACHER CONFERENCES?

As in any case, being prepared with the proper items leads to a successful and productive meeting. Consider the following items to be essential in terms of their presence for every conference: a schedule of individual conference times, a ruler, pens, pencils, writing paper, a highlighter pen, and individual student work sample files. The individual work sample files will serve as the focal point of the conference and should include the following in this correct order: (1) a current individual student grade printout, (2) copies of all in-class tests given to that point, (3) handwritten work samples, and (4) the most current results of individual student standardized test scores.

I suggest having the following items present as well for certain conferences: the school calendar, your personal planning calendar, class book, copies of prescribed content standards, course outlines, weekly lesson plans, parent communication log, classroom assignment log, copies of all assignment templates, a complete listing of future due dates, any individual education plans (IEPs), a file of the most recently received but not yet graded or recorded makeup work, and a timer. There are also personal items that you will find helpful that include water, snacks, breath mints, throat lozenges, and a laptop computer and books for reading for any times that parents may not arrive for a scheduled conference.

As always, keep in mind that a significant amount of due process lies in providing advance notice to parents, students, and administrators for everything and keeping complete documentation to support your positions. Before any conference or meeting, a teacher should survey the materials they will have before them and ask themselves two questions: (1) Am I prepared to give a valid answer for any question that I may be asked? (2) Do I have empirical evidence to support my answer when I respond? Again, preparation is the key. As with any task, you should plan thoroughly and carefully for all possible situations that may arise during parent conferences just as one would for any other professional meeting.

HOW CAN A CORE SUBJECT MATTER TEACHER SET STRATEGIES FOR PARENT–TEACHER CONFERENCES?

- Remember in advance that nature has provided parents with a strong emotional attachment to their child. This factor will be the strongest dynamic in any parent–teacher conference. Consequently,

since a parent may see all things related to their child's experiences through this subjective lens, it is of paramount importance that you project yourself, and any analyses that you provide, from the perspective of an objective and caring professional.
- Take the lead in the conference by welcoming the parents and offering some positive words about their student.
- Keep your contributions to the dialogue objective rather than subjective; keep all dialogue sequenced, focused, relevant, and to a minimum. Do not overtalk the process.
- Address the three main areas of attendance, academic performance, and citizenship in that order. Remember, what is desired, but not of paramount importance, is that the parents leave happy. What is of paramount importance is that the parents have the exact truth about their child's school performance.
- Regarding recorded absences: if a discrepancy exists between your record and the parent's recollection of their child's whereabouts on a day in question, a quick check of any assignment recorded on that date may reveal that the student has no recorded score. This would help serve to validate your records.
- Regarding academic performance: it is essential to have the student's work sample file present to share with the parents. The file should have the following items in this order:

1. The state and district content standards for your course's subject matter. The rationale here is that some prescribed state and/or district curricula may contain component parts that some individual parents may take issue with and want to do so with you during their conference time. Politely acknowledge their concerns and remind them that teachers do not set the curriculum. Attempt to redirect them to administration for discussion regarding curricular matters later. Make every effort to keep the time focused on the individual student's performance.
2. A course outline with accompanying class rules.
3. An individual student's computer grade printout chronologically listing all assignments given, date that each assignment was due and recorded with yellow highlighted lines for each missing or not passing assignments, and the course grade as it currently stands.

4. Copies of all tests given since the beginning of the grading period. Understandably, parents do not like to see anything on their child's tests but As. If any test score falls into the sub-A category, it is common for parents to ask, "What date was this test given and what day of the week was that?" When the teacher responds with the needed information it is also common for parents to indicate that their child did not study for that or any other test the night before. If a teacher provides the generous option of correcting test mistakes for the minimum grade of C or offering test retakes and the child under scrutiny had previously declined the teacher's offer, this becomes apparent when the work sample file comes under review.
5. A good work sample file includes at least one writing sample by each student, preferably in the student's own handwriting as opposed to being completed on a computer. Compositions in the child's own handwriting tend to provide parents with a revelatory experience in many cases.
6. Any other documentation that you deem relevant and helpful to the conference.
7. The heart and summit of the conference comes with the next document in the work sample file: the student's most recent standardized test scores. For teachers of core classes, this document can be used as a basis for comparison with the student's class assignment, tests, and projects grade printout. Comparing these two documents can tell quite a story for both teachers and parents. If class grades and performance are congruent with standardized test performances, the basis of future strategies can be easily set for remediation or acceleration. If class grades and performance exceed standardized test performance, perhaps praise is in order for both student and parent for hard work and determination. If class grade and performance lag behind individual standardized test performance, a motivational deficiency may be identified and indicates the need for a prescribed and specific course of action by parent and child.

- Address citizenship third in the sequence. If the student being discussed is a model of exemplary citizenship, let it be known to the parents and consider the moment a prime opportunity to make that the highlight of the conference. If the student being discussed

has a pattern of suboptimal behavior, let it be known to the parents as well, using only phrases limited to the objective expression of events observed.
- At this juncture, expect the parent(s) to ask the following type of questions:

  1. How does my child know what is expected of them?
  2. How does my child know what the classroom rules are?
  3. How does my child know what work has been assigned?
  4. How does my child know when assignments are due?
  5. Is my child participating in class?
  6. What extra help is my child getting and when is it available?
  7. Explain what you meant during Back to School Night and on your classroom website when you said . . .
  8. And any possible questions that could be considered as a cross-examination so as to find some opening for assigning culpability to you for their child's in-class issues. Many parents are quite skilled, especially in the middle school years and beyond due to extensive practice, in playing the game of "gotcha." If you allow the slightest unanswered opening for this line of questioning, you should expect to be considered 100 percent at fault. You should prepare accordingly.

- To assist you in answering any possible questions that parents may ask at this point, quick and easy access to the supporting documentation of the school calendar, your personal planning calendar, your class book, additional copies of prescribed content standards, course outlines, past weekly lesson plans, parent communication log, classroom assignment log, copies of all assignment templates, a complete listing of future due dates, any individual education plans (IEPs), a file of the most recently received but not yet graded or recorded makeup work, and a timer may be of great assistance.
- End the conference with cordiality by including some complimentary words about the student. Kind words can have a big impact in every case.

WHAT STRATEGIES EXIST FOR PROBLEMATIC PARENT–TEACHER CONFERENCES?

The overwhelming majority of parent–teacher conferences will be quick, amicable, productive, and what we in the profession might term "high five conferences." However, on occasion, unproductive and/or problematic parent conferences may occur and present themselves in one of five quite predictable forms. First, it is not uncommon for a conference to be completed by a parent only in a perfunctory manner as if it is just another obligation to be checked off the to-do list. Second, the parents involved may be experiencing some degree of unresolved feelings between themselves that have a spillover effect during the conference. Third, an attempt at triangulation may occur in which parents may express their dissatisfaction with another teacher or administrator in your building or another building. Fourth, a triangulation attempt may involve a set of parents where one parent may support you on an issue while the other parent may not. During conferences of the sort, stay professional and focused on what matters and what the time has been designated for—and that is the student. Fifth, there is always the possibility that a parent may become confrontational.

If you ever find yourself participating in a conference that does not seem to be going in a positive direction, first remain calm and professional and do not let yourself be baited into becoming a participant in any emotional exchange. Do not attempt to create any immediate remedy for the sake of keeping the peace. Remain focused on the issues at hand, great or small, and attempt to bring a truncated conclusion to the conference after all required and relevant information has been shared on your part. A great exit strategy is to explain to the parents that there is an overriding need for the conferences to remain on schedule so all parents have their full scheduled time and that you would like to continue the discussion further on another appointed date. This is one time when a timer may be a welcome conference tool. Bringing even a temporary end to the scheduled conference will allow a teacher added time to strategize for a successful resolution and the parents added time to reflect on their concern and consequent style of expression. If you feel the need, do not hesitate at any point to seek an available administrator to join in the conference and then yield to the administrator's lead from that point.

If you have a scheduled conference with a given parent who has a history of obstreperous conference behavior and one you do not feel comfortable dialoguing with one on one, do not hesitate to enlist the presence in advance of an administrator, department chairperson or grade level leader at the conference. You might also suggest a "staffing" conference with all the student's teachers present in lieu of an individual conference. In the most unlikely event you are spontaneously confronted by a parent or student who is exhibiting confrontational and/or aggressive behavior, do not engage them in discussion but request immediate assistance from administration.

FINAL THOUGHTS REGARDING PARENT–TEACHER CONFERENCES

Remember, teachers are professionals and need to take the lead in keeping conferences well planned, objective, document rich, and focused. Address attendance, academic performance, and citizenship in that order. Always interject as many positive observations as you can about the student. If it is necessary to share a given student's problem behavior with parents, keep your comments limited to examples that are observable and the frequency to which they occur. As always, a proactive mindset on your part, proper planning, and timely communication can help to mitigate problematic situations and may even prevent them before they occur. Specifically, if problematic behavior or underachieving academic performance comes to surface in the first week or two of the school year, you would be well advised to contact the parents immediately to at least make them aware of the problem and hopefully to acquire their assistance in finding a remedy for the undesirable situation. Under no circumstances should parents be initially informed of attendance, academic performance, and/or behavior issues at parent conferences in the month of November. You can expect a negative reaction from the parents and should be prepared to explain to them why they were not informed earlier. Implementing these suggested strategies will help ensure that both you and parents will have a productive conference experience that leads to ever-improving student performance.

QUESTIONS AND PRACTICES FOR CRITICAL THOUGHT

1. List and explain several reasons why school to home communication is important.
2. Hypothetically place yourself in an interview for a new teaching position. The principal asks you, "Please describe the ways in which you would communicate with parents concerning their child's attendance, academic performance, and citizenship. Be specific." How would you respond?
3. Hypothetically place yourself in the role of a parent attending the November school-wide parent–teacher conferences and meeting your child's teacher for the first time. The teacher informs you for the first time of your child's multiple failed examination scores, incidents of disrespect shown toward her and the other students, and current behavior that now can only be described as withdrawn while at school. Describe your feelings and thoughts about this news.
4. List and explain reasons why parent–teacher conferences should be greatly anticipated by teachers.
5. List and explain the steps of properly preparing for parent–teacher conferences.
6. Describe any strategies that you would have in place before meeting parents in a conference format.
7. Explain why it is important to anticipate the range of questions that parents may have for you during a conference.
8. Explain the role that standardized test scores can play in parent–teacher conferences.
9. Describe some strategies that could be employed for a problematic parent–teacher conference.

DEVELOPMENTAL ACTIVITY NUMBER 10

Select at least one person of your choice, preferably one or more fellow teachers, and conduct practice parent–teacher conferences. Remember to include all varieties of possible conference types in the series of practices. After each practice conference, make written notes about what went well, what needs improvement, how well you were satisfied with each conference. Since each conference you participate in over your career can truly be a learning experience, it will be beneficial to keep notes on what you continue to learn over time.

Chapter 11

Maintaining High Professional Standards

> Integrity is doing the right thing, even when no one is watching.
>
> —C. S. Lewis

As a teacher, you have been granted the public's trust, especially when it comes to the safety and general welfare of the public's children. The legal term *in loco parentis*, as mentioned in an earlier chapter, merits being called to mind once again. This is the Latin phrase for "in place of a parent," in reference to the legal authority granted to a person, such as a teacher, who takes on the responsibilities of a parent in the absence of that parent. This equates with the concept that every teacher must provide care for each student in their charge as if those children were their own children. Regarding professionalism and vigilance in the process of fulfilling these duties *in loco parentis*, if a teacher is to ever make an error concerning the health, safety, or mental or physical well-being of a student, that teacher must err only on the side of caution. Therefore, let it all begin by presenting yourself as a professional. A teacher who dresses as a professional, speaks in a professional manner, and conducts themselves as a professional inspires not only the confidence of parents, students, and colleagues, but in themselves as well. In this process, always keep a professional distance between yourself and others. When it comes to the students, and this cannot be overemphasized, you can never be a "friend" of any student in the sense of peer-to-peer friendship. Your role is limited in scope to serving as a supervisor, mentor, academic instructor, guidance counselor, and substitute parent. Equally important is that you be ever vigilant in the supervision of all students in your charge. Always keep every student in your field of view. If a student has been excused for a trip to the library, office, or restroom, make sure that you can account for that student by name, destination, and times excused and returned. You should perform a silent head count at random intervals, especially in the primary, intermediate, and middle school levels. Constantly be on the lookout for safety hazards such as holes in the playground or field surfaces or facility conditions that are in disrepair or could serve as a potential safety hazard. Report such conditions to the building principal immediately and keep a written record of all such activities.

HOW DOES A TEACHER HELP CREATE A GOOD RELATIONSHIP WITH ADMINISTRATION?

There is an old saying, "The boss isn't always right, but the boss is always the boss." Take this old and wise saying to heart. The first step in creating an excellent working relationship with your administrative team is to understand the chain of command and your place in that sequence. The voters give mandates to the state legislators, state and local school boards, who in turn provide direction to the district superintendents, who in turn provide direction to the building principals, and who in turn provide direction to the teachers. As a teacher, if questions, comments, or concerns about directives you have received arise, speak only to your direct supervisor/building principal. If a teacher should take a concern over a professional difference of opinion "over the principal's head" to the superintendent, then that teacher should not expect anything that may resemble a positive outcome.

There is an optimal level of interaction that should occur between a classroom teacher and a building principal. All teachers should make certain that administration clearly knows what their direction is in terms of philosophy, pedagogical techniques, and classroom climate. If a principal should be contacted by a parent with a concern, that principal will instantly be able to call to mind the context of your classroom and style. This enables the principal to be immediately able to speak to that parent from a well-defined frame of reference. Building administrators certainly value classroom teachers who are self-directed, teachers who avoid unnecessary consumption of an administrator's time, but they also value teachers who keep building administrators informed. If there is any incident that involves a teacher, the administration needs to hear about it first from that teacher rather than a parent or student.

There are certain habits that may be manifested among given faculty members that building principals do not value. Some examples include a teacher who

- Chronically complains.
- Attempts to "rearrange" the set administrative agenda by continually pushing for changes that the administration is not interested in.
- Is so convinced in what they believe is in the best interest of students that they would like to not only see the principal adopt their sense of curricular and instructional direction, but wants every teacher in the building to do so as well.
- Implements classroom policies that are chronically viewed by students and parents as procedurally and substantively unfair.
- Breaches student confidentiality and/or discusses school business with members of the community.
- Socializes with students.
- Fails to report any incident of suspected child abuse.

HOW DOES A TEACHER HELP CREATE A GOOD RELATIONSHIP WITH FELLOW TEACHERS?

It is important to spend lunchtimes, shared duties, and common meeting times in the company of fellow teachers. This helps to solidify a sense of common purpose and general camaraderie among colleagues. However, you should be watchful to avoid the frequently occurring and counterproductive faculty room gripe sessions. If necessary, attempt to redirect conversation to nonschool and/or positive topics. Like students, if teachers are using their valuable time wisely, their day will only include task activities.

FINAL THOUGHTS REGARDING MAINTAINING HIGH PROFESSIONAL STANDARDS

All teachers must conduct themselves with the same level of professionalism that they would expect from professionals in other fields. You should strive for a level of professionalism that will place you on the same plane as a physician, attorney, or judge. In so doing, you are certain to gain the respect you deserve from all quarters and be considered by many as the true professional you are.

QUESTIONS AND PRACTICES FOR CRITICAL THINKING

1. Define and explain the concept of *in loco parentis*. Further, explain the concept of holding the public's trust.
2. List and explain multiple ways in which a teacher can present as a true professional.
3. Interpret the phrase "keeping a professional distance." Explain the ways in which a teacher can keep a professional distance from students, parents, and colleagues.
4. Explain why the supervision of students always is of critical importance. Cite some practical examples of teachers providing supervision of students in their charge. Include both acceptable and unacceptable examples of student supervision. Further, explain why you consider each example as acceptable or unacceptable.
5. Define and explain the concept of "chain of command." Explain the placement of teachers in the chain of command in the educational environment.
6. From an administrative perspective, what are some teacher characteristics that principals value? What are some of the teacher characteristics that principals do not value?

DEVELOPMENT ACTIVITY NUMBER 11

Each state has a teacher licensing commission that sets standards for the issuance and renewal of individual teaching licenses. The mission of these commissions is to establish, uphold, and enforce professional standards of excellence and communicate those standards to the public and educators for the benefit of the students of each state. Unfortunately, there are instances where an individual teacher may fail to uphold and/or meet these set standards. If so, the teacher in question may be disciplined by their state's commission. These disciplinary measures range from a public reprimand to a license suspension, to even a license revocation. Want to know specifically what not to do as a teacher? Go to your state licensing agency's website and read the disciplinary/sanctions log and avoid these common lapses of professional judgment and behavior.

Chapter 12

The End of the School Year and Taking Care of Yourself

If you feel burnout setting in, if you feel demoralized and exhausted, it is best for the sake of everyone, to withdraw and restore yourself.

—Dalai Lama

WHAT ARE TYPICAL END OF THE SCHOOL YEAR RESPONSIBILITIES FOR TEACHERS?

At the end of the school year when all the students have gone home for the summer, it is your time to bring closure to the classroom's operation. Not only will you need to file the required paperwork with the main office, but you will also want to leave your assigned classroom better than you found it so that it is ready for you, or another teacher, to begin duties for the next academic year. Some items for attention include, but are not limited to, the following:

- File final grades and attendance for each student with the main office as required.
- Update cumulative folders for each student as required.
- Participate in meetings with colleagues to form class lists for the upcoming academic year.
- Complete and file a classroom supply inventory as required.
- Complete and file a classroom technology inventory as required.

- Complete and file a written request for teaching and classroom supplies for the upcoming academic year.
- Complete and file a consumable workbooks order for the upcoming academic year.
- Complete and file a list of any equipment repairs and work orders as needed.
- Make sure textbooks are cleaned, counted, stacked, and stowed.
- Clean, count, stack, and stow all student desks.
- Clean, count, stack, and stow all student chairs.
- Clean and clear all classroom shelves.
- Clean and clear classroom whiteboards and bulletin boards.
- Clean and clear classroom closets.
- Store classroom flags and similar room items.
- Return all materials borrowed from the faculty room, library, kitchen, office, etc.
- Remove all items from your office mailbox.
- Meet with the administration or their representatives for final checkout and signout.
- Attend any faculty luncheon and/or retirement ceremonies.

TAKING CARE OF YOURSELF

In general, teachers tend to be altruistic individuals. Too often their concern for others extends so far as to create an imbalance in their own lives that is characterized by being heavy on care for others while concurrently being light on care for themselves. Such zestful altruism, though admirable, may eventually result in the unintended and paradoxical result of providing a suboptimal experience for students. Simply stated, as a teacher, the demands on your inner resources may become greater than the supply of those inner resources. Most long-time veterans of the teaching profession will say that there are many incontestable realities that go along with classroom teaching. One of those realities is that the best interest of students and the best interest of teachers are inextricably connected. The simplest example is that a mentally and physically healthy teacher is much more effective than one who is out on stress-induced medical leave. Therefore, I suggest some areas of self-care that are important to your teaching performance and how, and ways that each can be addressed:

- Exercise: The benefits of exercise need no explanation. Always build some level of formal exercise into the already overcrowded day and feel comprehensively better for it for the next twenty-four hours. Even after teaching all day, even if followed by daily coaching or other extended responsibility, when student supervision responsibilities conclude, immediately go to the school weight room for a "speed" workout, start an after-school walking club on the school track, swim laps at the high school pool, stop at a local gym on the drive home, or plan for a quick home workout. If it is a more convenient arrangement, schedule a workout before school. At any rate, conventional wisdom among fitness enthusiasts holds that as long as you do some form of exercise each day, you are mentally and physically benefiting from it. This can be managed, and you can still be home on time for dinner, assisting with house responsibilities, or assisting with our own little kid's homework, bath time, bedtime, story time, and so on.
- Dietary Considerations and Moderation: Again, no explanation needed here. However, the way in which one wishes to address this category may vary from person to person. Being honest with yourself will only lead to one possible conclusion, and that is, your teaching performance is affected by what you put into your body. For people with blood sugar issues, what they eat and how often they must eat is an important consideration. Carbohydrates are a known source of needed energy, but if you consume a carb-heavy lunch, you might find yourself desperately craving sleep by midafternoon. Caffeine consumption is a factor as well. Perhaps one cup of coffee may make you more energetic in the morning, but more than that may possibly increase your irritability levels. An adult beverage while watching a professional sporting event on television after dinner may be appealing, but there is no chance that would enhance your next day's teaching performance. The old saying "listen to your body" applies.
- Hydration: The benefits of hydration are many, not the least of which are improving cognition and mood—both critical attributes to teacher performance. Water consumption for a classroom teacher,

depending on timing and amount, can become either a friend or foe. Say for instance a thirsty teacher drinks an entire liter of cool water right before teaching back-to-back ninety-three-minute high school block classes. Well, you get the idea.
- Sleep: Each person's sleep requirement varies, but the standard eight hours is recommended. Allowing yourself to become sleep deprived is not only a detriment to performance, but also dangerous to others as well.
- Interests Outside of the Profession: I highly recommend you establish as many personal interests as possible for evenings, weekends, and nonschool days. One colleague whose children were quite young at the time planned a series of weekly Sunday family outings that included activities like picnics, canoeing, bass fishing, hiking, bowling, movie matinees, museums, or anything out of the house that the entire family agreed upon. Not only did these activities have their own intrinsic value, but they also were effective in precluding the common "Sunday blues." As the kids grew up, she found additional hobbies such as pleasure reading, gardening, cooking, and musical interests.

FINAL THOUGHTS CONCERNING TAKING CARE OF YOURSELF

It is my sincere hope that what I have shared in this book will result in the enhanced development of the organizational and pedagogical skills of many teachers. Further, I hope that this intended organizational and skill development in teachers is then transformed into something even greater and more valuable—the improved learning outcomes of many students. Together, when these two aims become realized, so many greater accomplishments can and will follow. Best wishes for all your teaching days!

Appendix

Scenarios for Reflection

A wise principal once said that a school is a microcosm of society. As we all know, society can occasionally be characterized by pernicious behaviors, ungraceful interactions, random happenings, and dilemmas. So if a school is indeed a microcosm of society, logic would correctly dictate that some of these same characteristics could describe events that may, from time to time, occur in a teacher's workday. After all, humans are just humans and not machines. Nevertheless, as any veteran teacher can tell you from experience gained through their service, teachers must care for and teach every student who comes through the school doors with patience and to the best of their abilities with no exceptions. They also know that they must follow all laws at all levels, respect the chain of command, maintain collegial relations, follow all prescribed protocols as outlined in the teacher's handbook, adhere to all codes of ethics and professionalism, and avoid sowing the seeds of discord. Since children are priceless and vulnerable, a teacher's margin for error in judgment is nonexistent for all practical purposes. Stated another way, the range of possible human behavior is unlimited, yet proper teacher actions in response are defined by very narrow parameters.

The following are real-world examples that demand a teacher's acknowledgment, judgment, and an on-the-spot decision concerning correct course of action. Place yourself in the given situation as a teacher facing such entropic scenarios and ask, "What would I do in this situation?"

Scenario #1: You teach two morning classes a day in a district elementary school, and you complete your teaching day with four late morning and afternoon classes in a middle school in the same district. You have been assigned after-school extended duty responsibilities as a coach for three middle school sports spanning the entire school year. Both of your assigned schools conduct mandatory weekly faculty meetings after school on the same day and at the same time. Consequently, you do not attend faculty meetings at either school, but receive the meeting minutes for both faculty meetings in your box in the main office each week. In your annual written evaluation, both principals who supervise your work have given you superior ratings in all categories, except you find that the elementary principal has, without notice, marked you down for (1) not attending after-school elementary school faculty meetings and (2) not being present for the elementary after-school pickup car line. You explain that your middle school coaching and student supervision responsibilities preclude your ability to be in two places at the same time. The elementary principal expresses indifference to your response and the single category downgrade remains in your evaluation. What would you do?

Scenario #2: A student is earning a high A in your class, then misses week three and four of the current grading period due to illness. Consequently, the student's grade has dropped to a D+ at the time midterm grade reports are set to be sent out to parents. The school's grading software only allows for A through F grades on midterm reports. Upon receipt of the midterm report the student's parents request an after-school conference with you to discuss the existing situation. What would you do?

Scenario #3: You are teaching an advanced math class of high achieving students. Generally, in-class test scores and class grades run high. However, year after year, most students have trouble with the chapter 10 test and score poorly. Recognizing the need to reteach the chapter material, you spend extra time in class reviewing the test questions and answers, working out all the proper steps to solve each test question on the board, and requiring the students to make the necessary corrections to the errors on their respective tests. Historically, this has proven to be sufficient before moving on to the next chapter. However, one parent arrives before school without an appointment and *emphatically* demands that you formally reteach the chapter. Reteaching chapter 10 would create a time crunch vis-à-vis the school calendar, most likely causing the final chapter in the textbook to go untaught before the school year ends. What would you do?

Scenario #4: You are returning corrected, graded, and recorded assignments to the students while they are doing routine seatwork. One student who did not receive a returned assignment asks, "Where is my assignment?" You remind them that they did not turn in that assignment; therefore, you do not have one to return. The student then replies in a loud and indignant tone, "I turned that in, and you lost it!" What would you do?

Scenario #5: You are a teacher in a large comprehensive high school. It is your planning period, and you are returning to your classroom after checking your mailbox in the office. In the hallway you encounter a student with a shop class injury. He has run a power saw blade deep into his hand between his thumb and index finger and is bleeding heavily. You assist him to the school nurse's office, but it is locked and she has gone home for the day. What would you do?

Scenario #6: It is lunchtime, and you have cafeteria duty followed immediately by playground duty. You are allowed your thirty-minute duty-free lunch after these responsibilities are complete. The building principal supervises a daily "lunch bunch" detention in your classroom while you are on lunch duty elsewhere. Upon returning to your classroom after the bell rings sending students back to class, you realize that a major food fight has occurred in your classroom. Spaghetti noodles are hanging from the light fixtures, meatballs have struck the walls leaving sauce splatters everywhere, and bread and lettuce bits cover the floor. What would you do?

Scenario #7: Weeks after being assigned, the due date has finally arrived for a major term project that the students have been working on in class and at home. During the class turn-in procedure, one student registers a loud protest claiming during an emotional meltdown, "But you never told us that it was due today!" Later during the day, you receive an email from that student's mother that she would like an afternoon conference with you regarding this matter. What would you do?

Scenario #8: You have been told in confidence by her counselor that one of your sophomore students is pregnant. During period 3 in a subsequent morning class, she has a spontaneous and major episode of morning sickness in the classroom before even being able to leave from her assigned seat. What would you do?

Scenario #9: A student calls you by your first name in class. You remind the student(s) that you are properly addressed with the prefix Mr./Ms./Mrs. Later, while on hall duty, the same student refers to you again by your first name, only this time the principal is present. What would you do?

Scenario #10: You are leaving the school building late at night after an evening program. You appear to be the last one out—except you encounter one female student sitting against a hallway wall, knees pulled up to her chest, head down, and crying. You remind her that it is time to go home, but seeing she is obviously emotional, you ask her what's wrong. She responds through her tears that she just cannot go home one more time because her dad beats her up. What would you do?

Scenario #11: You are teaching a large class of remedial math students. You are reviewing material with which the students appear to be having difficulty. While you are rigorously explaining the mathematical order of operations on the board, three young male students stand up and spontaneously break into a beautiful three-part a cappella version of "The Lion Sleeps Tonight." What would you do?

Scenario #12: You go to a fellow teacher's classroom seeking some information regarding some school matter. Upon greeting him, you notice his thermos bottle sitting on his desk and his presence has the distinct odor of alcohol. What would you do?

Scenario #13: The principal calls your classroom on the school phone system. He informs you that he has received a bomb threat phone call. He then directs you to leave your classroom and check the restrooms on your floor for anything suspicious and report back to him. What would you do?

Scenario #14: You are on duty in a very long ground-floor hallway the last period of the day. As usual, the closer it gets to the bell ending the school day, you see teachers having difficulty keeping students in their classrooms. Suddenly, the distant exterior entry doors are being held open by two male students to allow a student to enter the building on a motorcycle. The motorcycle loudly and rapidly is approaching your position. What would you do?

Scenario #15: You have given a language arts writing assignment regarding a recent novel the class has finished. While reading and then writing comments on the student papers you received, you take notice that one female student has randomly inserted a paragraph about her mom's boyfriend behaving inappropriately toward her. What would you do?

Scenario #16: You are on elementary school playground recess duty. You are alone since your duty teacher partner has not yet shown up. At the far end of the playground, you see an unknown adult male entering the area appearing to seek a shortcut across school grounds. What would you do?

Scenario #17: After returning to your classroom at the conclusion of lunch recess there is a routine fire drill. As your students depart the classroom single file, you conduct a headcount with all present and accounted for. Upon arrival at the designated staging area, you again conduct a headcount only to find two students are now unaccounted for. What would you do?

Scenario #18: Your school conducts a lockdown drill. As per standard operating procedure, teachers have received no advanced notice of the drill. You direct your students to the proper positioning in the classroom, instruct them to be silent, check the hallway for any students to bring into your classroom, lock the door, and close the blinds. Several of the students cannot stop nervous giggling. You remind them in a soft tone that silence is important. Eventually, an administrator speaks over the public address system that the threat has passed and to return to normal classroom instruction. What would you do?

Scenario #19: The tardy bell has rung and class begins, yet a small group of your students have their phones out and appear to be sharing a text and having a giggle fest. They seem impervious to your directive to put their phones away since they are so humored by the text they are reading. What would you do?

Scenario #20: On your way to the office to check your mailbox during your planning period, you encounter a father/parent who appears to be very angry. He walks directly toward you, and you are forced to step aside to avoid a collision as he heads into the school office. You are aware that he is a former police officer and that he has had friction with the school's administration in the past. You notice that he has a holstered handgun on his belt that is in clear view. What would you do?

Scenario #21: The building principal says that he considers cell phones to be legitimate online learning tools and are acceptable in classrooms. Students in your classes have their eyes invariably glued to their phones. What would you do?

Scenario #22: A new principal arrives the next academic year and says that cell phones are not allowed in class and must be confiscated. What would you do?

Scenario #23: You are at one of the busiest times of the school year and you decide that you need to arrive in your classroom at 7 am daily to keep up with your workload. Routinely, the very nice teacher next door comes into your classroom during your early bird work time and jabbers your ears off until the 8:10 bell rings when students enter your room. What would you do?

Scenario #24: A fellow teacher is out for the day due to illness. There are not enough substitute teachers in the district that day to cover the number of absent teachers. The principal respectfully and regretfully asks you to cover one of the absent teacher's ninety-three-minute block classes during your planning period. For the good of the order, you consent to the principal's request. The absent teacher has not left any written lesson plans except for a sticky note directing any substitute to show a particular Hollywood produced video. You start the video only to realize that it is wildly inappropriate to be shown in any PK–12 classroom. Your judgment demands that you immediately discontinue the showing of this video. You now have ninety minutes of class time to cover without a lesson plan or even any suggested direction. What would you do?

Scenario #25: You arrive at school in the morning to begin your teaching day. On your approach to the school building, you notice that a Mercedes has crashed into the gate of a seasonally empty community swimming pool in a park area that is on school grounds. The auto is now resting on the bottom of the pool. What would you do?

Index

504 Plans, 11, 23, 17, 23, 52

academic calendar, 20; academic master calendar, 20
academic performance, 93
accommodations, 11
achievement gap, 10, 13
ad hominin fallacy, 12
administration, 11
administrator–teacher communications, 104
Advanced Placement, 50, 78
The Analects of Confucius, 46
annual teaching evaluation, 2, 24
annual written goals, 24
appeal to common belief, 12
application, 65
assemblies, 26
assessment, 4
assignment log, 57
assignment template, 98
attendance, 93; and late work policy, 3
auditory learners, 81
audio-video library, 20

Bell, Alexander Graham, 45
bell schedule, 23
Berra, Yogi, 75
biases, 10
Bloom, Benjamin, 7
book fair, 27
building maintenance, 24
bulletin board, 20

calculus, 78
CALM Daily Lesson Plan, 63–78
car line pick-up, 24
Carlyle, Thomas, 78
chain of command, 104
chemistry class, 56
child abuse, 105
child safety training, 17
child welfare service, 79
citizenship, 97
Class Activity Lesson Matrix, 63, 72
class book (binder), 23
class lists, 109
classroom: assignment log, 98; book library, 19; climate policies, 2, 4, 5, 6, 7; safety, 52
class service project, 24

cognitive biases, 15
collaborative activities, 65
community, 9
comprehension, 65
conceptual reinforcement, 65
content standards, 47, 96–98
Cornwell, J. M., ix
Counsel for Economic Education, 34
counselor(s), 11, 17
course outlines, 2, 20, 49, 54, 98
CPR training, 17
critical thinking skills, 65
cultural differences, 9, 13
cumulative folders, 10, 109
curriculum, 4
curriculum-instruction-evaluation, 33

Dali Lama, 109
demographic data, 10
department meetings, 17
Dewey, John, 6
dietary considerations, 111
differentiated instruction, 81
Direct Instruction Activities, 63, 64
dismal science, 78
dismissal book, 24
District Content Standards, 20
due process, 57

Einstein, Albert, 9
Elder, Larry, 55
emergency procedures, 23
end of school year responsibilities, 109
English Composition and Literature, 48
equipment and room repairs, 110
essential instructional tools, 40
exercise, 111

faculty meetings, 17
fallacy of composition, 12, 13

first aid training, 17
Ford, Henry, 86
four phases of planning sequence, 40
Franklin, Benjamin, 17, 39
future due dates, 98

Gardner, Howard, 7
grade level meetings, 17
grading periods, 27

hands on activities, 66
handwriting samples, 97
higher education, 10
higher order tasks, 65
historiography project, 56
Homer, 46
Homework Activities, 63, 65

IEP, 11, 17, 23, 52, 81, 98
in loco parentis, 1, 103
in-service week, 17, 18
instruction, 4; instructional best practices, 3, 41, 42
interactive, 65
interruptions 81
interscholastic economic competition, 78
IT Specialist, 24, 31

job interviews, 2, 5, 30; job application materials, 2
Jog-a-Thon 25
journal writing, 72

Knight, Bobby, 33

Landry, Tom, 63
late work policies, 3
learning: assessment, 64, 68, 70, 71; closure activity, 65, 66, 69, 71; environment, 76; essentials, 64, 66, 67, 70; modalities, 80, 81;

Index

objectives, 50; starter, 64, 66, 71; styles, 81; target, 64, 66, 73; theory, 56
lesson design, 56
lesson plans, 40; contingency lesson plans, 53; daily lesson plan model, 55; lesson planning book, 20; quality weekly lesson plan template, 56; teacher lesson plan book, 56; weekly lesson plans, 30, 55, 98; year-long lesson plan, 45, 46, 54
Lewis, C. S., 103
license renewal, 21
linear alignment of curriculum, 3
local school boards, 33, 34
locker assignments, 24
logbook, 19, 30, 31
logical fallacies, 12

Malthus, Thomas, 78
mandatory reporters, 79; suspected child abuse, 79
master contract (bargaining agreement), 23
models of instruction, 55
models of teaching, 56
Montessori, Maria, 7

National Content Standards, 20
National Counsel for Teachers of English, 34

off-task student behavior, 40
online class page, 57
organizational steps, 19
outside interests, 111

Parent Back to School Night, 2, 25, 30
parent communication, 9; parent communication log, 98
parent teacher conferences, 27, 93–99: preparation, 94–102; problematic parent–teacher conference strategies, 99; strategies, 99
parts of speech, 69
pedagogy, 55
personal philosophy of instruction, 1, 2, 3, 5, 7
personal planning calendar, 98
Piaget, Jean, 7
picture day, 25
portfolios, 21, 22, 30
post hoc fallacy, 12
Preliminary Activities, 63, 64
presentation skills, 3
pre-test–instruction–post-test, 35
principals, 104
problematic student performance, 93
professional deportment, 103
professional development, 17; professional development units, 21, 23
professional hardcopy toolkit, 56

red herring fallacy, 12
research skills, 3
room parents, 26

safety hazards, 104
seating chart, 23
self-care, 110
shadow days, 25
Skinner, B. F., 7
sleep, 111
socio-political ethos, 13
special education, 11
standardized testing, 34, 39; standardized test scores, 10, 95
state and local school boards, 104; state boards of education, 34; state departments of education, 34

State Content Standards, 20
Student Accommodations and Support, 52
student body elections, 25
student centered class activities, 3
student grade printout, 96
student management techniques, 56
student supervision, 104
student work sample files, 96–97
superintendents, 104
supply inventory, 109–110; supply ordering, 110
syllabus, 2, 20
system template, 39

Talented and Gifted, 49
Teacher Edition textbook, 20
teacher orientation, 17
teaching schedule, 23
teacher to teacher communication, 105

team debate, 56
technology trainings, 17
transcript, 11
Turner, Nat, 93

U.S. Census Bureau, 15
United States Constitution, 47

visitation days, 25
visual learners, 81
Voltaire, Francois-Marie Arouet, 1, 6

water cycle, 66
weekly syllabus, 57
work sample file, 21
workshop Activities, 63, 65
writing skills, 3

zero week, 17, 30

About the Author

Mark A. Marchese, EdD, has forty-one years of teaching experience in social studies, language arts, mathematics, and science. His teaching assignments have ranged from the primary grades to the university level in both public and private schools. Dr. Marchese has received honored educator awards from the University of Arizona, Clark Honors College at the University of Oregon, Portland State University, and St. Anthony Elementary and Middle School. He is currently an adjunct clinical faculty member at George Fox University.

www.ingramcontent.com/pod-product-compliance
Lightning Source LLC
Chambersburg PA
CBHW020334170426
43200CB00006B/380